A Burglar's life; or, The stirring adventures of the great English burglar Mark Jeffrey; a thrilling history of the dark days of convictism in Australia

James Lester Burke, J E Heiner, W Heiner

A Burglar's Life

OR THE

STIRRING ADVENTURES OF THE GREAT ENGLISH BURGLAR

MARK JEFFREY

A THRILLING HISTORY OF THE DARK DAYS OF CONVICTISM IN AUSTRALIA.

PUBLISHER :

ALEXANDER McCUBBIN

MELBOURNE

PREFACE

----o----

Who does not know Mark Jeffrey, or "Big Mark," as he is generally called? His well-known form is seen day after day, in wet and dry weather, as he limps along with the assistance of two stout sticks, on business bent always Though he lives at the Launceston Invalid Depot —an asylum for the indigent aged—he is not an idler, he earns what he can by honest peddling, turning over a shilling here and a shilling there But what a life has been his! What trials, sins and wretchedness he has passed through! A chequered life, truly! One full of incident and adventure, and, alas! one full of sin and wickedness Let the following pages be a warning to the young generation Many may read them whose lives are cast in happier conditions than his, but to them he would say that they might learn by a perusal of the incidents in his life a lesson of patience under afflictions, which are but as dust compared with those which embittered his life, and reduced him to the condition of a cripple in his old age Truly it can be said that his temper was the cause of a great deal of his wretchedness, but uneducated, untutored as he was, and without proper friends to guide him his mind became warped and diseased, and his temper uncontrollable Under happier circumstances, Mark Jeffrey would have made his name famous, as it happened, his life has been wasted May his closing years be happier than those which have passed! He is bright in spirits, his manner is now quiet and subdued, and when visitors call to see him he chats very genially of his past experiences The following pages are written in Mark's own language, with very few alterations Though illiterate, he is a man of sound sense, and has a keen insight into human nature He possesses, moreover, a remarkable fluency of speech, and those who call upon him will be well entertained by his personal narrations, of which he retains a firm grasp

A BURGLAR'S LIFE

———o———

CHAPTER I

Birth—My Parents—Early Days—Running Away From Home—Ely Fair—Hawking—Boxing and Bad Company—An Elopement and Its Consequences—A Battle to the Bitter End.

I was born at Wood Ditton, near Newmarket, Cambridgeshire, on the 31st day of August, 1825, so that I am now in my 68th year

My father was an industrious gardener, and resided at my native place, having rented a house and some three or four acres of land from Dr Norton, of Newmarket Part of this he had converted into an orchard, and the remainder he generally laid down with vegetables He was accustomed to go out reaping and mowing in the seasons, accompanied by my brothers and myself, and by these means he accumulated certain money, which he put by till he had sufficient to purchase two houses, besides making additions to the place he rented My father was also in the service of Dr Norton for eighteen or twenty years, but after the decease of the doctor, the whole of the estate was sold, including my fathers' residence After this occurrence, my father became addicted to drink, gradually squandering not only the money he had saved in times of prosperity, but also the proceeds of the two houses he had purchased, until eventually his growing sons were left very much to their own resources Having obtained, owing to mowing and haymaking seasons, a knowledge of the countries adjoining Cambridgeshire, and, moreover, being a rather sharp boy for my years, I decided to leave the parental roof and seek my fortune In forming this resolution, I was actuated chiefly by the changed character of my father, whose reverses caused him whilst under the influence of drink, to beat us most unmercifully

In 1840, being then only fifteen years of age, I ran away from home, taking my brother Luke with me, he being three years younger than myself

The first place we made a stay at was the town of Ely, where we met a party of gentlemen who, hearing our story, gave us as much money as paid for our supper, bed, and breakfast, and left us a few shillings to help us further on the road The following morning we left for the Fen country, halting at a Mr Jones's, at Heapshell

Hill, where we had formerly been in the habit of working with our father in the busy time of harvest It was in the first month of Autumn (September) that we arrived in the Fen country, and as the crops in this locality are generally late, the farmer put us two boys on reaping, and when this work was completed, he decided to retain our services and pay us off when the horse-bean harvest closed

During the horse-bean harvest a man known by the soubriquet of "Wicksty Riddles" was also employed thereat He was an inveterate drinker, and with the money daily obtained from Mr Jones, he would visit the public house, about half a mile off, invariably returning in the evening in a beastly state of intoxication His wages being spent in this unsubstantial manner, he had not the wherewithal to purchase food, and was wholly dependent upon my brother Luke and myself for the staff of life, in return for which Wicksty would tell us such stories of his experience as were likely to tickle our faculties

Having expressed our intention to proceed to Ely fair when harvest was over, Wicksty desired us to give him a sovereign, and he would put us in the way of earning a good living as Cheap Jacks This he was well able to do, he being at that time one of the best Cheap Jacks travelling throughout all England We boys laughed at him in this instance, and as he was almost bare of clothing, hinted that he stood in greater need of being placed in the way of obtaining not only the means of sustenance, but also garments to clothe himself So strongly did we scout the proposal, that Wicksty did not at that time pursue the subject any further, but it was destined to be brought more prominently before us in the near future

At the end of the harvest Mr Jones paid us off, my brother and myself being entitled to receive between us the respectable sum of £14 odd This amount had been partly raised by the provident manner in which we had lived during our sojourn on the farm The servants were on friendly terms with us, and supplied us with the greater portion of the surplus food that came from our master's table, to the great reduction of our maintenance bill We, moreover, slept in the barn of a night, covered with horse cloths and sacks, which further reduced our expenditure

On receiving our wages, Luke and I started off for Ely fair Having arrived at the town of Ely, we made inquiries for lodgings, and were referred to a Mrs Langford's Strangely enough, this was the very place Wicksty had recommended to us, probably in the hope of again meeting with us boys We, however, paid no heed to this coincidence We interviewed Mrs Langford, and eventually agreed to the exclusive tenancy of a room at 5/- per week We were to provide our own food, but our landlady expressed her willingness to cook for us, and on those terms we agreed to remain for a week

During our stay under this roof we first became acquainted with what is known in the old country as a "padding ken" Here it was the heterogeneous mass of the lame, the halt, and the blind of both sexes, congregated and slept without any partitions or regard to decency

On the night before the fair, Wicksty made his appearance at our lodging house in a state of intoxication After his admission he created such a disturbance that our landlady placed him amongst the roughs, far enough removed from us to prevent him being a source of annoyance

The fair at Ely usually lasted three days On the second day of the carnival my brother and I accidentally met Wicksty in the main street, he renewed his former overtures to initiate us into the business of Cheap Jacks, and we at length agreed to lay out five shillings on some articles, in order to learn whether we could obtain a living in the manner he described

Wicksty accompanied us to the swag shop—that is, the shop where goods are purchased wholesale by the Cheap Jacks—and asked the keeper of the shop for two razors at two and a half, knives, at three and a half, belts, at four and a half, and two pairs cotton braces at two and a half This was the system by which the goods were purchased up to eleven and a half, which signified pence We then accompanied Wicksty to an adjacent public house, where he sold the two razors, which we had bought for 2½d each, for the sum of 2/6, we thereby making 2/1 profit on those two articles alone By the exercise of a fluent tongue, he also managed to dispose of several of the other articles, on which he realised a proportionate profit

Stimulated by this success, my brother and myself agreed to co-operate with Wicksty, and it was eventually arranged that we should accompany our tutor through the adjoining counties Therefore, on the morning after the fair was closed, we all three went to the swag shop and purchased a stock-in-trade, consisting of knives, razors, belts, socks, women's stockings, sidecombs, tapes, trinkets, and needles, or as they are called in cant, "snells" On the last-mentioned article considerable profit was to be made The stock was purchased so cheaply, and allowed such a margin of profit, that many hawkers cleared from £2 to £3 per day in the speculation

Our first journey was in the direction of Lincolnshire, and by calling at the various farm houses, we managed to dispose of a considerable portion of our goods at a very large profit We always contrived to reach a large town each night, for the purpose of obtaining the best possible accommodation, and as we were making money very fast, we were not slow to pay for it Wicksty, however, proved a source of much trouble to us Almost

every morning we had to furnish him with the means for
a fresh start, as he would persist in getting drunk each
night, and spending the money he had made during the
day After the lapse of a few months, when we had
become thoroughly acquainted with the business of a
Cheap Jack, we deemed it advisable to part company
with Wicksty on account of his intemperate habits

My brother and myself now made our way through that
portion of country known as the Lincolnshire marshes,
until we reached the Yorkshire wolds In both places we
reaped good profits in disposing of horsehair, and we
gradually became possessed of a large sum of money.
The horsehair we obtained chiefly at the farm houses in
exchange for articles of cutlery and clothing, and it sold
readily in the large market towns through which we
passed—the short hair for 8d, and long hair for 1/- per
lb —so that our margin of profit was large indeed.

In the month of October, 1841, we arrived in Lancashire
after having travelled through most of the north-western
counties of England I was then a little over sixteen
years of age, and my brother and myself had a nice little
capital—between £40 and £50—with which to continue
the business of Cheap Jacks

Having at length arrived in Manchester, we each purchased a suit of the most fashionable fit and style, so that
we might more freely move amongst the better class of
travellers, and also for the purpose of gaining admission
into the company of other hawkers, from whom much
necessary and profitable information was to be obtained.

At this time we had no license to hawk goods, and to
prevent any undesirable interruption to our business, I
procured a license, which cost £4, and my brother Luke
agreed to act as my man, or paid servant. After carrying on business in the city of Manchester for eight or
nine months, we extended our operations to the suburbs,
and continued to reap a handsome profit on the sale of
our goods

Possessing from my boyhood a keen admiration for the
art of boxing, and having moreover a lithe and powerful
frame, I soon made my debut in many of the boxing
saloons which abounded in Manchester It was in these
places that I became acquainted with that class of persons whose company eventually proved ruinous to me—
such as sharpers, thimble-riggers, three-card men, and
others of a like description. Thrown into constant
relationship with them, my brother and myself spent our
money freely in their company We also became addicted
to the habit of drinking, though we exercised sufficient
control over ourselves to avoid becoming intoxicated

It was not until the latter end of 1842 that we shook
ourselves free from the vices and temptations of Manchester, and resumed our former nomadic life We retraced our way to Lincolnshire, and continued on till we
arrived at Hull, in Yorkshire, trafficking through the
various towns of this country until about the middle

of 1844 About this time we commenced to make boxing a part of our business, as both Luke and myself had become rather proficient in the use of our fists

At the latter end of 1844 we arrived at the hardware town of Sheffield There we visited the different manufactories, and replenished our stock to the best advantage After a short stay in Sheffield we struck across the country for our native place—Wood Ditton—which we reached in the early part of 1845. So much had we improved in appearance during our absence from home that none of our former acquaintances appeared to recognise us Luke was about 5ft 8in high, and weighed nearly 13st, while I was fully 6ft in height, and weighed 15st within a few pounds

On making enquiries whether our parents were still living at Newmarket, we learned that our father still resided there, although absent from home at the time of our visit, and that my mother had eloped with a single man named William Surridge She had been driven to take this step by the ill-treatment of my father Having news of the fugitives, he followed them, but we were informed that he had not been successful in overtaking them.

Our sister Tamar, who was younger than my brother Luke, was then in service at Newmarket, whilst our eldest sister Emily was housekeeper for Lady Cotton, at St Ives, Huntingdonshire, having several servants under her John, our youngest brother, had accompanied our father in his search, and William, who was the eldest son, was a sergeant in the Royal Marines, stationed at Chatham I may state that our family consisted of two daughters and four sons, at this time, the first fruits of my parent's union—a son—having died in infancy

As we could ascertain no definite intelligence as to the whereabouts of our parents, we resumed our hawking in the neighbouring towns and villages, and still continued to reap a high percentage of profit. We eventually made our way to Soame, near Lynn (Norfolk), where we had a rich married aunt, named Morley, who was my father's sister On enquiring if she could give us any information about our parents, we learned that our father had passed through there, but she could not enlighten us as to the whereabouts of our mother After a short stay at the town of Wisbeach, we made our way to Holbridge, in Lincolnshire I arranged with Luke to separately work the farms about the Lincolnshire marshes, and to meet in Holbridge each evening to report progress, and prepare an outline of our course on the ensuing day

On the day following our arrival, however, I met Luke about four miles from Holbridge, when to my astonishment he informed me that he had seen our mother at one of the cottages he had called at on his rounds, and that she was living with Surridge

He agreed to go to a public house, which was situated about a mile from the cottage, on the following day We did so, and Luke remained there, while I went on to try and obtain a conversation with our mother From the description Luke had given me, I had no difficulty in recognising the cottage by the piggery and a large patch of potatoes in front of the house My mother answered my knock, and she at once recognised me She asked me to step inside, and whilst I was revolving in my mind whether I should comply with her request or not, Surridge came to the door and also invited me in to dinner I entered the house, but I refused to take dinner with them I was undecided as to the course of action I should adopt, whether to call Surridge to account inside the cottage or entice him to the public house, and there seek an explanation I at length decided to have an interview with my mother in the first place, and she agreed to accompany me to the public house where my brother Luke was waiting my return

Having arrived inside, she consented to take a glass of ale with us, and I then led her into conversation

I ascertained that Surridge was known under the alias of Reid, by which name I will now call him I then asked my mother how long she had been cohabiting with Reid, and she replied about three years

"How does he behave to you?" I said

"Sometimes he beats me," she answered, "and at other times he is all right with me It is when the drink is in him that he ill-treats me"

I then told my mother that she would have to leave Reid and stay at the public house, that my brother and myself were able and willing to keep her, and that if she did not part with Reid, I would put an end to him

Whilst we were still conversing, Reid came in and asked my mother whether she would have anything to drink

"No," she replied, "I am not going against my son's wishes, and I do not intend to have anything further to do with you"

Reid then began to call my mother disgusting names, upon which I said to him —

"If you call my mother any more such names—although you represent yourself as a fighting man—I will give you the greatest trouncing you ever had in the whole course of your life! I will take all the fighting out of you!"

Some of those in the hotel who were acquainted with Reid urged him on to fight

"Get up and have a 'go in' at him," one shouted "Although he is a strapping young fellow we have seen you 'take it out' of bigger men than he, and perhaps you can 'leather' him also"

Without more delay, however, I asked Reid whether he would fight me in the house, or would he rather go outside, and he expressed a preference for the latter

Reid was thirty years of age, and about 12st weight He had the reputation of being a most determined fighter, and _____ he was defeated

On proceeding outside, one of the bystanders volunteered to second Reid

"I'll keep time, Mark," my brother Luke rejoined. "You need no seconder for the like of him!"

On that we both stripped and confronted each other, and it was here that I found the science which I had learned in the boxing saloons of Manchester stood me in good stead Reid made several ineffectual attempts to hit me, until at last, gaining an opening, I gave him his quietus by a blow on the throat, which he did not recover from for about ten minutes

My mother, although she did not interfere further, screamed out, "Oh! he has killed Surridge" (calling him by his proper name) "My son Mark will be hanged!" Time was called on several occasions, but it was some time before Reid got up and resumed the fight, when I at once gave him a blow on each cheek, which cut him very much, and caused him to bleed profusely The force of the blows felled him to the ground, and his head came in contact with a loose stone, so that he was unable to rise for more than five minutes

Reid, however, was undaunted, and on returning to consciousness, fought for about a quarter of an hour longer, when I succeeded in catching him under the short rib, and thus put an end to the mill My opponent was then conveyed home by some of the neighbours in a cart, and Luke and myself escorted our mother to the cottage, in order to obtain her clothing, prior to removing her in safety from the clutches of her unlawful protector

---

CHAPTER II.

En Passant—Cheap Jacks—Bad Company—Separation—Navvying—A Battle With a Yorkshireman—Notoriety.

Before continuing my narrative, I may here express a hope that the reader will not find these details of my younger days too fulsome or tedious My main desire in tracing them thus minutely, is to show how varied and unsettled was my mode of existence from boyhood upwards, to point out how early I was cast upon my own resources, and exposed to trials and temptations; and to give some crude idea of how I gradually became involved in vice and crime Therefore, if these preliminary chapters are void of interest to any of my readers, I sincerely trust that this explanation will be an all-sufficient apology for my lack of literary tact and experience

On the day following the fistic encounter narrated in the previous chapter, we retraced our footsteps towards Wisbeach, accompanied by our mother, whom we had induced to learn the business of a Cheap Jack She afterwards became very expert in that line, and succeeded financially beyond our highest expectations

From Wisbeach we made for Lynn and other towns in Norfolk, taking the country villages on our way, until we arrived at the city of Norwich .Our usual good fortune deserted us on this journey, for the county of Norfolk was at this time in a very poor and miserable condition After a brief stay at Norwich, we renewed our stock, and struck through the county of Suffolk. We remained for some time in the town of Bury St Edmunds, and then, having replenished our stock, we harked back once more to Newmarket.   -

The day after we arrived at the latter place, we—mother, Luke and myself—paid another visit to Wood Ditton, our native place Our father's brother (Richard Jeffrey) who resided there, and for whose house we made, expressed much pleasure on seeing us, especially our mother. He made enquiries as to where we had met with her, but on that head we did not satisfy his inquisitiveness We also visited our Uncle William, who was also very glad to see us all, and made a great deal of us.

We stayed at Wood Ditton for a week, travelling and hawking our goods during the day through the neighbouring villages, and returning each evening to The Three Blackbirds public house, at Outward Ditton—half a mile from Wood Ditton—where we had secured accommodation

Our next move was to London, the world's great emporium, doing pretty well with our wares on the road Upon reaching the metropolis, we accepted an opportunity which immediately presented itself of adding to our capital by purchasing a stock of Spitafields handkerchiefs —silk, satin, and variegated—for 1/3 each, which we afterwards disposed of at from 5/- upwards, from which an estimate may be drawn of the huge profit shopkeepers must have made from this class of goods at that time On one occasion we paid a visit to Petticoat Lane, which was not a very safe locality in those days, as it abounded in pickpockets and footpads. The shops were mostly persided over by members of the Hebrew persuasion, whose manner of doing business may be imagined by the following experience we underwent —

On entering one of the shops in order to make some purchases, the keeper requested his daughter to bring some gin out for the "shentlemans and lady"—meaning our mother We each had a glass of the spirit, which was not only rich in flavour, but made us feel more amicably disposed towards the crafty dealer. Whilst partaking of this hospitality, however, he endeavoured to draw the blinds over the windows, in order to exclude the light from the articles he was about to offer for sale I objected to this step, and after a heated argument, succeeded in inducing him to raise them again He dis-

which had, no doubt, been stolen   I offered him 6d each for them, upon which he vented an outburst of wrath upon us

"Get out of my shop!" he exclaimed, excitedly   "Do you think I stole them?"

"No!" I replied instantly, "but probably you received them, knowing them to have been stolen, and they say 'the receiver is worse than the thief'"

He became somewhat mollified when he perceived I was inclined to be outspoken, and having requested us to return inside, he expressed his willingness to deal with us.

After a considerable display of goods, and much haggling, we succeeded in purchasing a number of superfine Indian silk handkerchiefs at 1/3 each, and were glad to depart from his threshhold so easily

On leaving London, we directed our footsteps towards Woolwich, calling at Deptford, Blackheath, and Greenwich   We remained in Woolwich for some time, and did good business.   We then started for Chatham—the depot at that time of the Royal Marines—to see our brother William, who, as I have already stated, was a sergeant in the corps   We found on our arrival, however, that he was on duty, and it was not until the evening that we saw him by appointment, when he expressed himself very pleased to see us, more particularly my mother, whom he had not seen for a very long time

From Chatham we travelled towards the Hundreds of Essex, crossing the Thames at Woolwich.   We made a halt for a couple of weeks at Southchurch, pursuing our business of hawking, and making some profits, so that we need not encroach upon our capital

After our stay at Southchurch we took across country to Buckinghamshire and Northamptonshire, eventually resting in the town of Northampton for a few weeks.   We next visited Peterborough fair—a distance of forty miles from Northampton—where we set up a stall for the carnival   When the fair opened, I acted as Cheap Jack, Luke and our mother taking the articles to the various purchasers, and we did a remarkably good business

We stayed at Peterborough for two or three months, being accommodated at a respectable house where licensed hawkers and the better class of travellers put up   During our stay in this town we made the acquaintance of two young men named John and Thomas Hart, natives of the town of Bedford, who were hawking brooms and brushes, and also ornaments of every description   Our acquaintanceship with these two men gradually ripened into a warm friendship, and they eventually became closely linked in our career in crime   Of an evening they accompanied Luke and myself to the boxing saloons, but we could not persuade either of them to put on the mittens   We two brothers, however, were passionately fond of a set-to, and lost no opportunity of improving our prowess

One evening while I was having a friendly bout with a man named Martin Lloyd, a dispute arose, and a purse of £10 was made up for Lloyd to fight me I backed myself for a similar amount to win, and Martin agreed to fight for the money in the boxing saloon We fought only five rounds, during the last of which I gave Lloyd a blow that caused him to throw up the sponge

As our acquaintanceship with the Harts increased, I became extremely anxious as to terms on which Luke stood with Tom Hart They appeared to avoid my company, and did not return home until the night was well-nigh spent This caused me much uneasiness, as I feared that, Luke would be led into serious mischief by his companion I therefore took the opportunity of pointing out to him the probable results of his conduct, and was glad to perceive that my mild rebuke and advice were received in a true spirit by him It led to a separation between the Harts and ourselves, and we agreed to journey forward once again on our own account

My mother also left us at this juncture, as she had obtained a situation with a lady in another part of England On leaving us, she offered to present us with her stock, and also the money she had saved, but we refused to accept either, as we were then in comfortable circumstances

Luke and myself then started towards the North of England, reaching Kendal, in Westmoreland, about the latter end of 1846 A railway was in course of construction at this place, and we remained in the locality about two months, drinking and associating with the flashest and worst company we possibly could After spending most of our ready cash, and also parting with a large quantity of our goods, we made for the railway line, and sought employment On getting into conversation with one of the gangers named Dan Barton, I discovered that he was from the same county as ourselves (Cambridgeshire) He told us we could start work with him on Sunday morning (the men worked Sundays as well as week days), at 5/- per shift of eight hours, and that if we chose we could make 14 shifts per week I, however, objected to work on Sundays, and he arranged that we should start on Mondays, and make 12 shifts per week

On commencing work on the Monday, the ganger put us into a very easy run, on account of us being townies, and because many of the men who had received their month's pay on the previous Saturday were away on the spree.

A few days afterwards, a big Yorkshireman came to where I was working and demanded what business I had on his run

"If you do not get off it," he exclaimed, "I'll give you 'Lankay' for it—I'll kick the head off you!"

I told him to see the ganger about it, as I would not quit my position unless Barton told me to do so

He continued to provoke me, until at length I challenged him to a level spot, assuring him that I would give him enough to keep him from going on a run for some time to come

However, many of those who were working near called out to me —" Don't hit him, young fellow, if you do you'll be fined five shillings, let it be till dinner time "

The Yorkshireman agreed to wait till dinner time, rejoining —" I'll fight ye ' Lankay ' fashion! I'll bite yer nose off! I'll kick ye! I'll punce ye!" But as I did not approve of the Lancashire method of fighting, I objected to fight him that style, and expressed a desire to have a fair stand-up battle

At length we came to an agreement, which stipulated, among several other things, that we were not to wear any boots Whilst I was stooping down unlacing those articles, the big Yorkshireman struck me cowardly on the ear, felling me to the ground The men loudly resented his conduct, and compelled him to wait until I was in fighting attitude When that time arrived I had my revenge, for I knocked him to the ground two or three times in succession, which compelled " Yorkey " to cry for quarter and relinquish the fight

This brought me notoriety, and I became known all along the line as " Big Mark," the hawker and fighting man, an appellation which I have vere since maintained.

When my brother and myself received our monthly wages we placed it carefully by to recoup ourselves for the money we had foolishly squandered in debauchery, and make a fresh start in our own particular line of business We had £12 each to draw monthly, and after paying for food and lodgings, and other incidental expenses, we were enabled to save £8 each out of our wages

We also added to our savings by giving lessons in boxing on pay nights to our fellow workmen. For this purpose we erected a tent and stage, and our project took immensely well The majority of the navvies were young men, and they welcomed the opportunity to become acquainted with the noble art with much enthusiasm

Nor was this our only means of adding to the earnings won by legitimate labour on the railway, for by degrees we laid in a stock of clothing and useful articles, which we traded with to the satisfaction both of ourselves and our purchasers

CHAPTER III

Seeing Life—Fun With the Women—Jealousy and Its Results—A Cowardly Foe—Knocked Out—Marked for Life—A Lenient Ganger.

The course of events ran smoothly enough until the third pay night, when Luke and I, being desirous of witnessing some fun amongst the men and "smallgang," mingled with a crowd that was wending its way to a public house known by the sign of the Bird-in-Hand. We found plenty to amuse and interest us, and did not think of returning home until the hour of closing By that time we were both in an advanced state of intoxication for the first time in our lives Halting for a short rest in a lane midway between the public house and our lodgings, the influence of the drink we had imbibed so benumbed our faculties that we both drifted into a drunken sleep, from which we were aroused at an early hour on the following morning by a policeman, who ordered us to get home

I started in affright at the position in which he had found us, for I had little recollection of the concluding part of our evening's carousal. I remembered, however, that when we had set out from our lodgings, I had a large sum of money in my trousers pockets, a portion of which belonged to my brother Luke, and my hand instinctively wandered in search of it To my great dismay, it was not to be found in any of my pockets, and we at once concluded that I had been robbed Fortunately, however, such was not the case, for a few minutes afterwards, whilst Luke and I were giving the policeman such necessary information as might have led to its recovery—allowing that we had been robbed—I was overjoyed to find that I had maintained sufficient control over my faculties to have secreted the money in an inner cavity of my waistcoat

This led to a renewal of our drinking bout, for we at once offered to treat the constable on the strength of our good fortune The limb of the law was nothing loth to comply with our offer, and he escorted us to the sign of the Elephant and Castle, where he succeeded in rousing the landlord from his bed Although the host was not inclined to forsake his couch at that early hour, he supplied us with a bottle of brandy, glasses, and water, and gave us permission to enjoy ourselves in comfort in an adjacent outhouse The policeman remained with us until the hour arrived for him to report and go off duty, by which time he exhibited no uncertain signs of the brandy being overproof Luke and I remained in the outhouse until the inmates of the public house were astir, when we entered and each engaged a bed

After a refreshing sleep and a substantial dinner, we spent the afternoon by dancing and capering with two German women who had come in—one having a barrel organ, and the other a tambourine Not only could my brother and myself sing a passable song, but I possessed the art of mimicry to a considerable degree, therefore our impromptu entertainment had the double effect of pleasing the patrons of the house and stimulating the business We remained in the house that night, and succeeded in becoming on good terms with the landlord

After breakfast on the following morning, feeling in no way disposed to return to our employment, we remained in the public house drinking and dancing.

On this occasion we paid court to two of the servant women, both of whom were pretty and fascinating I succeeded in making considerable impression on the affections of my partner, much to the chagrin and discomfiture of a master tailor, who was her humble and ardent wooer She paid no heed either to the protestations or implorations of the love-sick knight of the goose, until the infidelity of his idol caused him to drown his manhood in tears, and he rushed madly from the room amidst a whirlwind of badinage and laughter

That evening, much to the relief of our landlady, we returned to our lodgings The good woman had been much concerned as to our safety, for she was aware that we had gone out with a large amount of money in our possession, and she believed both of us to be steady and temperate men Firmly convinced that we had been waylaid and injured, for the purpose of robbery, she had strongly secured our room—which contained a large stock of goods—in anticipation of a visit from the robbers

Early next day, feeling the same disinclination for work, and being still infatuated by the charms of the servant women, we betook ourselves once more to the Elephant and Castle The astute landlord greeted us cordially, and, as privileged customers, ushered us into the parlour, where most of the quality was sitting We, however, did not remain long in this apartment, for we found the bar-room and our female associates of the previous day more congenial to our enjoyment, especially as the itinerant female musicians had returned.

During the afternoon a big Yorkshireman, who was a ganger on the line, came in I then found that the tailor was not the only rival I had to contend with for the heart and hand of the buxom servant woman to whom I was paying homage, for the Yorkshireman was also an aspiring suitor I also discovered, however, that she was not altogether unmindful of me, for upon the Yorkshireman endeavouring to engage her attention, she abruptly rejected his overtures, remarking that she did not want to have anything to say to him, and that I was the man she wanted for a husband

At this the Yorkshireman grew furious, and advancing towards me he said, in broad Yorkshire dialect, " Tha an' me will have it oot i' th' yard."

The landlord, who had overheard the conversation, called me into the parlour, and stated that as Luke and I had been spending our money freely, he would not like to see us get into any bother He advised me not to fight the Yorkshireman, as he was a dangerous opponent, and came from a part of Yorkshire where they were accustomed to fight in a style called "up and down"

I, however, turned a deaf ear to his advice, for my temper was aroused I assured him that I had fought other men with a reputation similar to that of the Yorkshireman, and had got the best of them

I challenged my opponent into the yard, and, accepting my invitation, we immediately stripped for the fray, in which I was assisted by my brother Perceiving, on the opening of the encounter, that the Yorkshireman was deficient of science I contented myself by walking round him and keeping him at bay, intent only on tiring him out At length I feinted with the left, and got in my right on the throat of my antagonist—a favourite hit of mine—which felled him to the ground, where he lay for some time in a helpless condition

I turned to my brother and the others who were standing round with the remark, "That is six months in the hospital, but the next blow will be sudden death!" Hardly had I uttered the words, however, when my opponent rose suddenly from the ground, and catching hold of me unawares by the legs, threw me in turn to mother earth Scarcely had I fallen prone when he gave me three kicks with his heavy boots, two of which opened my nose, and the other split my head Yorkey's boots, I may remark, were not only heavy, but had iron toe-plates as well I was rendered unconscious, and my brother Luke immediately went in search of a doctor The bystanders meanwhile were so exasperated at the cowardly conduct of my opponent, that they laid hands on him and gave him a most unmerciful thrashing Everyone that could get within arm's length of him took part in this act of retribution, using not only their hands but their feet as well

When the medical functionary arrived, he sewed up the splits in my nose, dressed my head, and put forth his efforts to restore me to consciousness The wounds are plainly perceptible even to this day, so that I will carry the trace of this cowardly action to my grave

Luke assisted me into the public house, where I was put to bed, but at my own request, I was eventually removed by him to our lodgings My brother attended to my every want during my enforced confinement, for my eyes were so discoloured and my face so swollen that I was unable to return to my work

I had some misgivings that this affair would lower me in the estimation of Daniel Barton, our ganger, and perhaps be the means of causing Luke and me to lose our employment, so that when I was in some measure convalescent we waited on that individual Far from being

annoyed at the cause of our absence, he expressed much
sympathy towards me in my misfortune, and assured us
that we could make a fresh start as soon as we were
able and willing to do so.

———

CHAPTER IV

Travellers Once More—Bendigo Thompson—I'm "Off"
Fighting—A Gambling Mania—Bad Company—Raising the Wind—An Eventful Compact.

When Luke and I resumed work, we resolved to lead a
less vitiated life and add to the savings we had encroached
upon by debauchery   By dint of close persistence to our
work, and aided by the profits accruing from hawking
and boxing lessons, we were in possession of between
£300 and £400 in hand cash at the end of six months, in
addition to a large stock-in-trade

Luke and I now decided to resign our occupation on the
railway line, and devote our sole energies once again to
vending and selling as Cheap Jacks   With this object in
view, we purchased a horse and chaise cart from a man
who had been on the spree, for the sum of £30, the turn-
out being in reality worth £20 above that amount   We
subsequently purchased another horse which was a good
stamp of animal, for £10, using him as a leader, and driving in tandem fashion

Thus equipped, we made towards Manchester, as being
the most desirable place to replenish our stock of soft
goods, afterwards visiting Sheffield, where we purchased
a large quantity of cutlery 50 per cent lower than we
could have done at the swag-shops

Having by these means added to our stock, we pushed
towards the town of Derby, and we remained there for
two or three months, transacting a profitable business
with the navvies engaged on the line   Business at length
became rather flat, and we made our way through
Leicestershire, halting for some time in the town of
Leicester, and subsequently travelled onward through
Nottinghamshire to Nottingham

Here we remained a month or two, making the
acquaintance of a number of gamblers and pugilists, including old Bendigo Thompson, who was then ex-cham-
pion pugilist of England   "Bendy," as he was familiarly
termed, contracted a great friendship for me, and strove
his utmost to induce me to undergo a course of training
for the pugilistic ring   I was extremely averse to his
proposal, however, chiefly because I had a strong disinclination to earn my living in such a manner   Bendigo
had a number of smart pupils under his tuition, and I
expressed my willingness to have a bout with any of
them, without placing myself in training

One of these young fellows represented himself to be the "Tipton Slasher," but he, however, was not the real Simon Pure. Nevertheless he was not to be despised by any means, he being about 5 ft 10 in in height, and weighing about 14 or 15 stone. Slasher and myself often had a set-to of an evening with the gloves for pastime, and on one of these occasions he lost his temper, and threatened to wreak summary chastisement upon me. Thereupon I challenged him to fight, offering to stake £20 to his £10, with the further proviso that if I did not win the battle in twenty minutes I would willingly forfeit the stakes. Slasher, however, declined to accept the challenge.

So greatly did Bendigo's admiration for me increase, that he at length offered to take me under his fostering care for six months, free of all expense, stating that with such material he could teach me as much science as would eventually enable me to knock out the then champion of England (Ben Gaunt). He used every argument at his command to persuade me into undergoing the course he proposed, and told me I had the best staying power of any man he had ever come in contact with. But my resolution was inflexible, and I assured Bendigo that I had no desire to stand up before any of my fellow men, and run the risk of sustaining serious injury, unless in actual self-defence. Bendigo was extremely disappointed at my persistent refusal, for he doubtless saw in the natural skill I had been gifted with a means of enriching himself.

Luke and I made frequent visits to the many gambling saloons which existed in Nottingham, and thereby became on intimate terms with a number of bookmakers and gamblers, who obtained their livelihood by legitimate speculation on the turf, or by questionable pursuits. Through this circle of acquaintances, we were introduced into the society of a number of fast women of the better class, and, maintaining an intimate friendship with them, our business was neglected, and our capital rapidly melted away. Our lives were one constant round of gaiety and dissipation, and our companionship was much sought after whilst we were spending our money lavishly. I also had a weakness for driving my intimate friends about the streets of Nottingham in our vehicle, and on one of these occasions we met with an accident, by which several of my friends sustained serious injury; but, miraculously, Luke and I, as well as our horse and trap, escaped unscathed.

Through the total exhaustion of our exchequer, we were at length compelled to part with our horses and cart. We obtained £50 for the lot, and as the horses were in better fettle than when we bought them, the bargain was a windfall to the purchaser.

To still further strengthen our funds, we recommenced selling goods as Cheap Jacks. We sacrificed our stock at so   nightly surrounded by a large concourse of people, who eagerly sought to reap the benefit of our sale

We also succeeded in transacting business with a large shopkeeper, who purchased a quantity of jewellery, hardware, and soft goods from us for the sum of £220 The stock was actually worth £450, but in our desire to obtain money, we parted with it at 33 per cent under invoice price   .

Being thus in possession of a goodly amount of ready cash, we forsook our late friends by shaking the dust of Nottingham from off our feet, travelling through Cambridge to the town of St Ives

We had no sooner put up at an inn at the latter town, than to our great surprise we encountered Tom Hart, dressed in the extreme of fashion, but in a state of semi-intoxication He greeted us, and particularly Luke, most cordially Ascertaining that he was staying at the same inn as ourselves, we retired to a private room

"Well, Tom, you appear to have done well with your crocodiles [earthenware ornaments] judging by your appearances," I remarked to our newly-found acquaintance, as soon as we had seated ourselves.

Hart laughed mysteriusly for some time, and at length informed us in confidence that he had been burglarising with three London "gonniffs," but owing to a dispute over an equitable division of the spoil, he had parted from them It appeared that the stolen money amounted to £250 Hart's mates had handled the cash, and as he had only received £50 as his portion of the booty, he inferred that he had been bilked by his companions in crime, and, believing that there should be "honour amongst thieves," he decided to desert them. He also told us that he had come to St Ives for the purpose of meeting his brother John, who had been sentenced to twelve months' imprisonment for stealing a gold watch, the term expiring on that day

Tom painted a very rosy picture of a burglar's life, and recounted the many successes he had experienced without either becoming implicated or suspected. He proposed that Luke and I should join him and his brother, and so successfully did he dangle the gilded bait before us that we readily consented to his proposition

The morning following our agreement the three of us proceeded to the gaol to meet John Hart on his release. On his appearance we congratulated him on obtaining his freedom, and then escorted him to our inn, in order to mature our plans for future operations

CHAPTER V

The Beginning of the Burglaries—Ghostly Garments—
"If that Fellow Does Not Go Back to Bed a Bullett
Through Him"—The Servant Women Befriended—A
Successful Start

On leaving the town of St Ives, the four of us journeyed
to Cambridge, where we secretly purchased the implements essential to our nefarious designs

At my suggestion, we agreed to adopt a ghostly costume for the purpose of carrying out our operations, as I
imagined that it would have the effect of striking additional terror to the hearts of those with whom we came
in contact during our expeditions I, therefore, made
arrangements with a female to make the necessary
articles, which consisted of flowing white jumpers, long
white leggings with peaks to cover our shoes, and white
headcloths, with eyelet-holes for the eyes In addition
to this, we each purchased a pair of white cotton gloves,
so that there should be no incompleteness in our weird
appearance

It was mutually agreed upon that our first exploit should
be at the residence of a Mr Jones, who resided on a large
estate close to the ten mile bank, near Lynn, Norfolk I
possessed some knowledge of this place, having worked
on it during harvest time with my father, and was well
aware that Mr Jones kept a large quantity of gold, silver
and notes on the premises, from which he paid the hands
during harvest

This gentleman also kept from twenty to thirty hands
in constant employment, the married men receiving 12/-
per week, out of which sum they kept themselves in food,
whilst the single men received £10 per year and board
Their wages, however, were greatly augmented during
harvest time, when they worked additional hours for extra
pay The permanent hands were allowed a bushel of malt
and a peck of hops during the harvest for the purpose of
making beer, whilst the casual hands were each allowed a
gallon of the best brew, half-a-gallon of ale, and as much
table-beer as they could drink The wheat grown on the
estate averaged between 30 and 40 bushels per acre, the
oats and barley from 50 to 60 bushels, and the horse-
beans also bore a heavy crop

We travelled towards this locality, and halted at a place
called Little Port, which was about four to five miles from
the residence of Mr. Jones It was then arranged that I
should shoulder my pack, and make my way to the house,
so as to be better enabled to "sound the crib" (examine
the premises) without raising suspicion

On the following morning, therefore, I set out, travelling along as if bent on legitimate business, and disposing
of my wares to those who were inclined to purchase them.
By means of careful questioning, I obtained some in-

formation anent the estate of Mr Jones, which very much
disheartened me, and made me doubt the profitable out-
come of our plot In the first place, I ascertained that
Mr Jones had been dead about four months, also that
Mrs Jones had discharged all the farm labourers but one,
and, further, that the house and estate were advertised for
sale or to be let on lease Truly, this was not a tempting
place on which to make our maiden effort!

Nothing daunted, however, I gradually made my way
towards the house, and was successful in obtaining an
opportunity of displaying my goods before the mistress
She purchased several articles of dress and jewellery from
me, after which I requested her to supply me with some
refreshment, notifying my willingness to pay She immediately bade the servant-woman to take me into the
kitchen and give me something to eat and drink This was
all I desired, for my object was to obtain some information as to the situation of the rooms Whilst doing
justice to the repast spread before me, I made myself extremely sociable to the servant women, eventually pre-
senting each of them with a pair of side-combs, earrings,
a wedding ring in anticipation of their future marriage,
and a sovereign By the exercise of a little conversational
tact, and keeping my eyes open, I gained all the information I required On bidding the servants good-bye, I
asked them if they thought they would recognise me
again and they replied they would not forget me, and
that they hoped to meet me at some future time, a wish
they unconsciously had speedily fulfilled

I returned to my companions at Little Port, and reported progress It was arranged that we should make
the attack upon the house at midnight, and we accordingly
reached the scene of operations about an hour before that
time We donned our ghostly habiliments in one of the
adjacent outbuildings, I, meanwhile, giving my companions some information regarding the situation of the
rooms I explained to them that the back door presented
the best means of access, it being secured simply by a
delicate lock and a small bolt, or, on the other hand, a
pane of the back window could be removed by a diamond,
which would enable us to push aside the catch of the
window and so obtain admission that way

On the left hand side of the door there was a ladder
leading up to an attic over the kitchen, and in which the
servant man slept The kitchen led into the hall, on the
right-hand side of which was the sitting-room, and on
the left the parlour Further along the hall, and near to
the front entrance, the library was situated, at one end of
which a staircase led to the sleeping apartments On
reaching the staircase landing the first room on the
right was the bedroom of Mrs Jones and on the opposite
side the apartment of the servant women

Having described this much, and insisted that no violence was to be used either to the women or the man, we
made preparations to enter the house Our ingress was

not made in a manner befitting the dress we had assumed, for my brother and myself made a run at the back door, and burst it open with the force of our feet. We had little to fear from the inmates, however, and the costume was worn chiefly as a disguise on this occasion. We left John Hart, or "Turpin, 'outside, watching the windows of the room occupied by Mrs Jones, but we failed to place a guard over the attic window of the man servant, not thinking for a moment that he would escape that way, it being a considerable height from the ground

The noise we made in effecting our entrance had disturbed the man, and placed him on the defensive. With one hand he was endeavouring to draw the ladder into his room, and in the other he held a pistol pointed at us, which we subsequently found to be unloaded

"Langham!" I shouted on observing the attitude of the man, "draw your pistol, and if that fellow does not go back to bed put a bullet through him!"

No sooner had I uttered the words than the man disappeared from the opening. Half divining his object, a moment afterwards I told my brother to go outside and watch the attic window while I ascended to the room. He did so, and came back immediately with the intelligence that the man had jumped from the window, and was making his escape. It was impossible to rectify our carelessness by this time, and so we set about our further operations more expeditiously, dreading that the escaped man would return with assistance

Entering the library, we found the staircase door leading from thence to the sleeping apartments was fastened on the inside. We seized the poker from the fireplace, and inserted it between the cracks or jambs of the door until we were enabled to get our hands inside and pull it open.

On getting upstairs we made for the room occupied by Mrs Jones, whom we found lying in the bed quite calm and apparently unconcerned. We assured her that we would not molest her in any way provided she produced what money she had in her possesion, and, after a little demur, she told us all she had in the house was under her pillow. We searched there and found a bunch of keys and a purse containing a £5 note, ten sovereigns, and a few shillings in silver

Leaving Mrs Jones in security, and taking the purse and keys with us, we proceeded to the servant girls' room, effecting an entrance by a spank of the foot. They were very much startled on perceiving four men entering their room, but we did our best to reassure them. We inquired of them whether they knew where their mistress kept her cash, but they replied in the negative. We then asked them if they had any money, and they replied they had not, with the exception of a sovereign each, which had been presented to them by a kind hawker during the morning. The women also said that their parents were in distressed circumstances, and in order to relieve them, they sent home what money they could spare from their wages.

The servants had apparently failed to recognise my voice, and upon leaving the room, I presented each of them with a five-pound note of my own money, requesting them to forward the amount to their respective parents.

After watching several other rooms, we came upon an apartment used as a dressing-room by Mrs. Jones. Here we were fortunate enough to discover a cash-box, which, on being opened, was found to contain the respectable sum of £270 in gold and notes, as well as a quantity of silver.

There were also several articles of jewellery in the box, and this Tom Hart wished to carry away. I, however, raised an objection, reminding him that we had agreed when forming partnership to touch nothing but solid cash, and I intended to adhere to that resolution. Tom reluctantly gave in, although he doubtless found it a sore temptation to break the rules of our gang. Especially might this have been the case when we visited the plate-room on the ground floor, where we discovered gold and silver services and other articles, sufficient to have made a small fortune for a man. Nor did we touch the wardrobes upstairs, although one contained many costly dresses and the other many suits of clothing which had belonged to the deceased owner of the estate.

On leaving the plate-room, I left my companions downstairs and proceeded to the room occupied by Mrs. Jones. I at once restored her to freedom, and as I tendered her the keys, I remarked:—

"We have seen your plate, your jewellery, and your dresses, Mrs. Jones, but we have not displaced any of them; we have only taken hard cash. Before I leave you, however, I wish to give you a word of advice. You are now an old woman, without family ties. Dispose of your property to the best advantage, and distribute the proceeds—over and above what you will require during the remainder of your life—to the poor. That's what I do. I give away cash to those who are poorer than myself, and what I do not give away I squander."

Mrs. Jones made no reply to this well-meaning advice, and I left her in solitude to meditate on the sageness of it.

We then—becoming uneasy as to the movements of the servant man—hastily decamped with our spoil. Having doffed the white garments, we separated, the rendezvous being Little Port.

CHAPTER VI

A Division and a Separation—My Mother Grows Suspicious—An Evil Life—Little Hells—Gambling—The Suburb of Barnwell—Preparations for Another Burglary—We Again Succeed.

After having made a fair division of the money obtained from the house of Mrs Jones, we decided upon parting company, but agreed to meet again at a certain time and place in Cambridge

Luke and I shouldered our packs, with the object of disposing of our wares along the different routes we pursued This not only had the effect of causing suspicion to be diverted from us, but it gave us the opportunity of visiting and inspecting any place we should consider worth operating upon

We all met again in accordance with the appointment we had made, nothing of interest having transpired to any one of us during the brief separation Luke and I almost immediately disposed of our packs at a wholesale swag shop, and, being flush of cash, we did not hesitate to part with them at considerable loss Our next act was to send our mother £40 each She was still living at Wisbeach, in the capacity of companion to a lady, as mentioned in a previous chapter We requested her to accept the amount, as we could well afford it, and would shortly be in a position to forward her another substantial remittance A day or two afterwards a reply came addressed to myself In it my mother returned the money we had forwarded to her, stating that she did not require any monetary assistance, and that, moreover, she was afraid our wealth had been obtained dishonestly She also expressed her dread that I was becoming involved in mischief, and stated that if any harm or disgrace befel me it would be the means of breaking her heart

Accompanied by the Harts, Luke and I spent the major portion of our time in visiting the "little hells," boxing saloons, and "flash" houses, the latter being chiefly occupied by thieves and women of disreputable character Our desire was to see life, and enjoy ourselves, and to accomplish our aim we spent our money with unstinted hands My brother Luke was an experienced player at cards, he having been instructed in the manipulation of them by a London 'gonniff," for which tuition he had to pay a good round sum I was somewhat proficient at skittles and three up, whilst the Harts were also fond of gambling, so it is not to be wondered at that we became addicted to the vice more and more, although the boxing saloons remained the same source of attraction to Luke and me

We also paid frequent visits to the suburb of Barnwell, where women of questionable repute resorted

I may here mention that women of lewd character were not allowed to parade the streets of Cambridge, for which offence they were at once apprehended by the police, or men known as proctors The authorities of Barnwell, however, did not exercise such firmness, consequently these questionable characters had taken up extensive quarters in that direction They dressed with richness and taste, and many of them were reputed to be the mistresses of the collegians. This suburb possessed a potent charm for us, and we were never weary of sporting our figures in its vicinity

Indolence and dissipation at length made considerable inroad upon our ill-gotten gains, and it behoved us to adopt some means to replenish our coffers Owing to the success of our first expedition, it devolved on me to choose the scene of our second exploit, and we finally decided to try our fortune at the residence of a Mr Snazell, in Louth, Lincolnshire This was another estate on which I had worked during harvest time with my father, and I had a clear recollection that the cash-box, from which Mr Snazell paid his harvest hands, was kept in a cupboard in the drawing-room To secure this cash-box was the aim I had in view, trusting to good fortune to find it well stocked with notes or current coin of the realm

The house was of two storeys, containing four rooms and a kitchen on the ground floor and four rooms above There were also several outhouses and barns adjacent to the building, in which the casual farm labourers from Ireland slept

The four of us departed from Cambridge at irregular intervals and from different points, for the purpose of lulling suspicion, and also to avoid any clue whereby we might easily be traced

On arrival at Louth, the Harts put up at the Globe Inn, and Luke and I at the Rising Sun We did not remain inactive long, for we agreed to carry out our plan the very next evening

It was some three or four hours walk from Louth to the residence of Mr Snazell, and we started separately in good time in order to reach our destination at midnight The rendezvous was a cluster of wheat stacks at the rear of the house, where we once more assumed our weird disguise

On my advice, it was agreed that we should proceed to the kitchen, take one of the panes of glass from the window, throw back the catch, and so effect our entrance noiselessly It was necessary for us to take more precautionary measures than we did on our first undertaking ,for I was well aware that Mr Snazell and two grown-up athletic sons slept on the premises, in addition to the mistress and her two daughters Then the number of servants was a point for consideration, more especially as I had a faint idea that some of them were of the masculine gender.

Tom Hart was told off to the front of the house to watch the windows, and John Hart stood sentinel on the road to warn us of the approach of danger, whilst Luke and I were to ransack the premises Each of us had a pair of double-barreled pistols, and I instructed Luke to keep one ready for use in order to intimidate the inmates should occasion arise, but at the same time I warned him against exercising undue violence, unless we were either in danger of apprehension our lives were placed in jeopardy

Our entrance was effected quietly and with expedition, Luke being the first to enter through the window, closely followed by myself. I retained sufficient knowledge of the situation of the rooms to enable me to unhesitatingly lead the way to the drawing-room, where we arrived without alarm of interruption The cupboard was the immediate object of my attention, and to our great joy we found therein the article we so much coveted, and for which we were risking so much danger Our first movement now was to acquaint ourselves with the value of the contents of the box, in order to learn if it contained a sum sufficient to remunerate us for our risk, or whether it was necessary to prosecute our operations still further Fortunately, we possessed a skeleton key which fitted the lock, and we lost no time in examining our surreptitiously obtained booty

---

CHAPTER VII

A Good Haul—A Season of Success—Our Last Burglary —Fickle Fortune Deserts Us—The Police—My Evasion and Pursuit—Arrest of Tom Hart and My Brother—In the Meshes of the Law

The cash-box we secured at the residence of Mr Snazell contained no less a sum than £346 in notes and gold, and also a small amount in silver Fully satisfied with this good fortune, we effected our escape, and returned to our usual resort at Cambridge We then indulged in a round of dissipation, which very quickly had the effect of melting our wealth Drinking and fighting, sporting and gambling, carried on with even regularity for a short time, was a fitting incentive for other robberies In spending our money we were unselfish enough, as we valued very little our ill-gotten store We could get more, we thought, as easily as we had obtained the last ,and so did not trouble our minds much at our ever decreasing wealth

Nor was this supposition unfounded, for further exploits were carried out with uninterrupted success Our operations were principally directed towards those places I had worked at with my father during harvest time A retentive memory aided the keen perception I possessed in my boyhood, in recalling not only the construction of the various houses, but also the habits of the masters, and the number of servants we would prboably have to contend with, so that we were better able to mature our plans. Fortune smiled on us benignly at St. Ives, Northampton, the Yorkshire wolds, Lincolnshire, and other places. In Lincolnshire we were particularly successful, securing over £600 from the residence of a wealthy gentleman.

It may appear incredible to many that such large amounts were kept in comparative insecurity, but it must be borne in mind that the houses we plundered were isolated from cities and banking institutions, and that large numbers of Irish farm labourers were continually travelling to and fro, so that in meeting their just dues, the owners of the various estates had constant need of funds.

In the natural course of events, however, our good fortune deserted us, and we were overtaken by the consequences attendant upon our career in crime.

Towards the latter end of January, 1848, we formulated a plan to rob a farmer who resided at a village a few miles from Ely. We left the latter place for our destination on a Friday night. arranging to meet together on the following evening at 12 o'clock, in close proximity to the farmer's residence. Thither, then, we repaired, and the four of us met outside the building as appointed. We dressed ourselves in the spectral costume which had so effectively aided us in the past, and then made our dispositions for the burglary. I had previously ascertained that the man servant of the family slept in a room situated in the upper storey of the house. We entered through the window of the back kitchen, I being in advance of the others. The Harts agreed to go upstairs and tie the "gauger," as we called the servant, whilst Luke and I remained below to search for the plunder we desired. We entered a narrow doorway leading to the room where the farmer and his wife slept, and we had no sooner done so than we heard the farmer challenging us.

"What do you want? Who are you?" he shouted.

I ordered him to be quiet instantly, threatening to blow his brains out if he made any trouble for us. He had risen from his bed, but on my ordering him back he did not resist. To ensure safety, however, we tied him down with his wife and infant. He demanded again what we required, and I told him we wanted money.

I may state that this man was not the owner of the land, which was part of a large estate. He was, however, an extensive dealer in cattle, and as the market had been held on the previous day, we fully expected to have found money in the house. We were somewhat disappointed, therefore, when the farmer remarked with apparent sincerity, in answer to my question, "There is no cash here."

But words had no convincing power with us, and we at once commenced to institute a strict search. I had just succeeded in finding a few shillings, when my brother Luke whispered to me, "I've sprung a haul! Let us give the signal and make tracks!"

He had discovered the money in the inside pocket of an overcoat which was hanging up in the room, where it had apparently been since the farmer's return from market It amounted to £60, and consisted of four £10 and four £5 notes

We did not take an immediate departure, but demanded of our victim where he kept the provisions and grog He informed us, and we refreshed ourselves with a quantity of cold pork and sundry glasses of gin, a bottle of which spirit we each put in our pockets before we left the house.

Of course, we separated, agreeing to meet at a place called Bigglesworth, about fourteen miles from Cambridge I instructed my brother to go to a man to whom we usually sold our notes, for the reason that it was risky for us to pass them in the ordinary way, they being frequently numbered by their rightful owners Bowle was the name of the man with whom we traded, and he kept a hotel—the Hit or Miss, I think it was—at Sneeds He gave us £4 for every £5, taking a £1 for the risk of exchange Luke left us on his errand, and was accompanied by Tom Hart, whose brother remained in my company.

The two of us were going along the road towards Cambridge, when my companion suddenly exclaimed that he heard someone coming from behind us He seemed fully convinced that we were being pursued, and wanted to throw away the remaining £10 note he had in his possession from the robbery we had just committed, in order to avoid suspicion I endeavoured to reassure him, for I had begun to entertain doubts as to John's sanity. He was gradually losing the courage he had formerly possessed, which was either occasioned by the continual strain upon his nervous system, or by heavy drinking I told him it was not likely that the alarm could have been raised by that time, as we had left the family and servant tied in perfect security In order to still further assuage his uneasiness, I promised to change the note for him when we arrived at Cambridge

He usually changed his notes at a shop in Barnwell, where he formerly purchased the goods he hawked about the country

I changed John Hart's £10 note and also my own when we reached Barnwell, and then, having parted with my companion, went for accomodation to a hotel kept by a Mrs Bright, who was a great friend of mine She had a daughter named Lizzie, who had conceived so much affection for me that, during my hawking days, she had on more than one occasion absconded from home and accompanied me on my travels

On entering the parlour, I asked the landlady for Lizzie, informing her that we were going to be married. We chatted for a short time, and she then brought Lizzie in to me, and while we two were conversing, the Ely police, who had been looking for me in all directions, entered the parlour, but owing to my disguise they failed to recognise me. The dress I had on consisted of a white hat, white mackintosh, and white leggings. Not wishing to bring discredit on Mrs. Bright, I sought her out and informed her of the position in which I stood, and gave her to understand that it was for me the police were searching. I also gave her a £5 note—the remainder of my share of that evening's plunder—for Lizzie, at the same time placing her on her guard against passing it for a little time. Taking my leave, I promised to return in a short time, and marry Lizzie.

My footsteps were turned towards Bigglesworth, but on reaching the outskirts of Barnwell I obtained accommodation for the night at a roadside inn. As soon as the inmates were astir on the following morning, I partook of a hearty breakfast, and proceeded towards Bigglesworth, where I was to be rejoined by my three companions on the approaching Tuesday evening.

Having arrived at the Half-way House, I entered for the purpose of obtaining rest and refreshment. Being well-dressed, the buxom landlady greeted me as if I were a person of distinction, instead of a hunted fugitive, who was striving to elude the myrmidons of the law. She invited me into the best parlour which the hostelry boasted, but my unpolished nature led me to express a preference for the tap-room, from whence were wafted the sounds of maudlin revelry. On being ushered into the tap-room I called for a bottle of ale and some bread and cheese, which the landlady prevailed upon me to enjoy in quietness and with comfort in the dining-room. Having finished this frugal though refreshing repast, I re-entered the tap-room, where I was accosted by a drunken man with a fine Newfoundland dog, which he had evidently stolen. He pressed me to purchase the animal, and thinking it might prove serviceable, and also tend to avert suspicion, I bargained with him for five shillings and a gallon of ale for those in the tap-room. In order to persuade the dog to follow me, I fed him on toasted cheese, which so tickled his palate that he swore allegiance by leaping around me and licking my hands.

Shortly afterwards, accompanied by my dumb companion, I resumed my journey towards Bigglesworth, and having arrived there in safety, I put up at the place my companions had agreed upon—the Shoulder of Mutton public-house. The landlord took charge of my dog, and I entered the parlour and sat for some time drinking several glasses of gin. Perceiving the entrance of a stranger, I raised my eyes, and to my great surprise observed the public-house keeper at Sneeds, the man who, as I have previously mentioned, usually changed my brother's notes. Notwithstanding the disguise I wore, he recognised me, and upon acknowledging my identity he informed me that my brother Luke and Tom Hart had been arrested on suspicion of being concerned in the late burglary, but he could not tell me where the arrest had taken place.

Judge of my mortification, however, when he further stated that Luke had incriminated himself by wearing a ring which had been stolen from the premises, and Tom Hart by a Kingsman's silk handkerchief. It had been a distinct understanding between us that under no pretext was anything but solid cash to be taken, and, personally, I had always paid strict observance to this precautionary measure. Luke and Tom Hart, by their lack of judgment and breach of good faith, had doubly increased the danger of their own salutation, and also placed my freedom in extreme jeopardy. I saw how desirable it was that I should quit the public-house I was then in, for there was considerable likelihood that the appointment made with my companions in crime would leak out.

The landlord was a staunch sympathiser with men of our class, and transacted a good business with a large number of them. There was also a "padding ken" connected with the place, so that it will be perceived that neither he nor his house was above reproach. I knew, however, that I could entrust my secret to him with perfect confidence, and, having done this, I requested him to engage one of the travellers in the "padding ken" to proceed about twenty yards ahead of me on the road to Baldock, and intimate by signs the presence of the police, so that I could make good my retreat. For this service I tendered him a sovereign, half of which he was to give the man he engaged.

Even while we were deliberating on this arrangement, two of the Ely police came in, but my disguise was once more effective enough to keep me from their clutches. After a little persuasion on the part of the landlord to induce me to secrete myself in the house, he engaged the traveller to precede me through Bigglesworth, on the road to Baldock. We succeeded in passing through the town in safety, and, parting with my pioneer, I continued the journey in the company of my dog.

I had not proceeded far along the road, however, when I heard a horse and cart coming from behind me. I waited till it came up and then hailed the owner, asking him how far it was to Baldock. He must have been sadly frightened, for as I hung on the back of the cart awaiting his reply, he whipped his horse, which started off at full speed. I learned afterwards that this individual gave information that he had been stuck up by a tall man, who had with him a large Newfoundland dog. He really believed, so formidable did I appear, that I was going to rob him.

When I arrived at Baldock I went to a poor woman's house and asked where I could obtain accommodation.

The woman directed me to an inn, and as I perceived evidence in the house of extreme poverty and destitution, I threw down some money, which she accepted very thankfully. I could not regard misery without feeling a desire to render aid, even though at that time I was anxious for my own safety. Moreover, I was always lavish with my money, and invariably had plenty of it.

I went to the inn pointed out by the woman, and made arrangements for the accommodation of myself and my dog. After giving instructions to be called at an early hour in the morning, I had a few glasses of gin, and was shown to my room by one of the girls, who wanted me to leave my shoes outside in order that they might be cleaned. I was too careful to risk that, however, for I knew they would be identified if the law officers entered the house, owing to one of the shoes being considerably bulged out by a dislocated ankle.

I slept too long into the morning, and hastily dressing I left the hotel without taking any breakfast. I knew that the police would be out after me in all directions, and that they would probably trace my movements to Baldock in a very short time.

But I had even then unconsciously run the full length of my tether. Escape was in vain, for my good star had waned at last.

I had scarcely turned my back upon the hotel, when I heard the galloping of horses behind me, and I saw that any effort to avoid contact with them would prove futile. However, I determined not to yield without argument. I could not run, for, as I quickened my footsteps, I suddenly felt a sharp pain in the ankle I had dislocated when a youth.

When the sounds drew nearer, to my great dismay I beheld a cart in which were three policemen. As they approached me, one of them presented a pistol at my head.

"We arrest you on suspicion of having committed burglary," he shouted. "Don't attempt to escape, or I'll blow your brains out!"

"I am an honest hawker, and have my licence," I replied with an air of assumed indignation. "What right have you to go about arresting honest men?"

My line of conduct proved of no avail, and after some further argument I was compelled to get into the cart and was driven back to Baldock.

The policemen asked me the name of the inn where I had slept on the previous night and I saucily replied, "Don't ask questions; it will be time enough for me to make statements when I am placed before an impartial justice for examination."

When we arrived at Bigglesworth, I was asked if I knew the Shoulder of Mutton Hotel, but they could get nothing from me. Then they threatened to put me in the "cage" (as the watch-house was termed), but I emphatically declared that I would not enter it. As they renewed their threats, I grew fearfully excited, and threatened to "slog" the police.

Breaking from their grasp, I whipped off my coat, and defied them to approach. I expressed my willingness to go to the inn and remain there under their supervision, but I was strongly averse to entering their filthy cells.

The crowd, which had meanwhile gathered round, was evidently inclined to support me, for they shouted out that I was perfectly justified in my answers. I was only taken on suspicion, they said, and the police had no right to pester me.

"Let him stay at the hotel if he wishes!" they demanded, and to the hotel I was eventually taken. The position assigned to me there was not very comfortable, for I was handcuffed to a large settle in the tap-room, with two sentries over me. However, to counterbalance this discomfort, I sat near the fire and ate, drank, and made merry with my guards, who were nothing loth to be sociable at my expense.

CHAPTER VIII.

Committed for Trial—Mad Actions—A "Darling" Son—A Triator—Fifteen Years' Transportation—Milbank Prison—A Fatal Fright—Religious Mania—Insubordination—The "Black Hole"—Woolwich Hulks.

On the following morning I was escorted to Ely, a few miles from the house where our last burglary was committed, and in due course was brought before the magistrates. I then found that John Hart had been arrested in the meantime, for my three associates were also placed on trial at the same time. I was identified by one of the farm servants connected with the place we had robbed. He had had a conversation with me on the day previous to the burglary, when I was "sounding the crib" and gleaning information, and he recognised me again by the scar on my nose. The wife of the farmer also identified the gold ring which was found in my brother Luke's possession as one that had been stolen, and also the handkerchief which Tom Hart had worn. In addition to these articles, a watch was produced, and it was alleged that John Hart had taken this from the manservant. The result was that we were committed to take our trial at the next sittings of the Cambridge Assizes.

The excitement attendant upon my arrest and the trial had a very depressing effect upon me; in fact, my mind became for a time almost totally deranged. I was tortured by confinement—at being deprived of the sweets of liberty and enjoyment—and the rough, unsubstantial fare, after my former good living, irritated me beyond measure. As I dwelt in solitude on the discomforts of my new existence, my rage and hatred towards my gaolers became ungovernable, and I bore a stronger resemblance, in my impotent wrath, to a caged beast than to a human being.

From early boyhood I had been accustomed to comfort—and I may say luxury—and to have my every want supplied by a never-empty purse; therefore imprisonment and coarse food were the more tedious and harrassing to me.

Our fare was half a pound of bread per meal, and two or three ounces of meat per diem—a substantial repast, indeed, for a man of my size and stamina to subsist upon!

One day, when more than usually hungry and exasperated, I seized an additional piece of bread from the turnkey, as he was serving out the allowance.

"You have one piece," said he.

This was provocation enough for me in the condition I then was, and I immediately retaliated by knocking him down. For this act I was sentenced to three days solitary confinement.

After undergoing this punishment, the authorities placed a man—who was also awaiting his trial—in my cell, in the hope that he would tame my rugged nature by reading the Bible to me.

At that time I was extremely ignorant and uneducated—not even knowing the alphabet—and I looked upon the doctrines he espoused as romantic fairy tales. Moreover, I placed no reliance on the veracity of the man; I grew suspicious of him, and thought that he was taking advantage of my ignorance and filling my ears with nonsensical twaddle for his own amusement. Goaded by this impression one day, when the miracle he was explaining seemed more highly improbable than ever, I was stung to madness and vented my wrath upon him. For this offence I was arrested and received another sentence of solitary confinement.

To show the reader still further how savage my disposition was at this period of my career, I had no sooner been released from my last term of solitary, than I broke all the cell windows with a broomstick whilst exercising in the yard. For this act I was fastened to my bedstead for twenty-four hours, and restricted to my cell for three days on bread and water.

There was a very valuable bloodhound kept in the gaol, worth some hundreds of pounds, and he had been trained to patrol the yard in order to prevent the escape of prisoners. After I had broken the glass of the cell windows, he contracted a habit of putting his long nose through the iron bars, treating us at the same time to some blood-curdling baying. These horrible growls at length exasperated me to such an extent that one morning I seized an iron pot, and watching my opportunity, I struck the dog such a severe blow that his nose was cut through. The blow was a cruel one, but it had the effect of abating the nuisance, and from that time he was of no value whatever.

Shortly after this incident my mother came to see me, and took me "off the country," which means that she would supply me with special food at her own expense. At the time of her visit I was doing one of my customary terms of solitary. The cell in which I had been placed was near the lodge by which visitors entered, and I could plainly overhear the conversation which transpired.

My mother was informed that her son Mark was a "darling"; that he had smashed everything that came in his way; and that he had received special punishment for his acts.

Bad news for a mother to hear on entering prison.

We were then permitted to have a short conversation through the bars. I need not dwell on that painful and emotional interview; suffice it to say that it was fortunate for both of us that the time allowed was so very brief.

After I had served the term of solitary I was then undergoing, I became more subdued, especially as I was provided with whatever food I desired. This amendment, however, was not of lengthy duration, for on being upbraided by a clergyman named Mr. Bennett, before my trial came on, for having committed the burglary of which I was accused, I advised him not to draw hasty conclusions, and insulted him in such a manner that he was compelled to fly from my presence. For this I was placed in irons—a heavy pair and a light pair—so that I was securely prevented from exercising much violence for the time being.

When the time arrived for my trial, I was taken to court and placed in the dock without being relieved of these cruel encumberances. The judge, however, acted as my mediator, and refused to go on with the case until they had been removed.

Luke and I had secured the services of Mr. Hunt for a lawyer, and Mr. Prendergast as counsel. The latter was one of the most eminent men of that time in London.

The evidence against us was of a most conflicting character, but I fully expected to have been acquitted, for Mr. Prendergast, when addressing the court, pointed out a great number of discrepancies, and his speech caused considerable effect.

The reader may therefore faintly imagine my consternation and bitterness when the under-governor of Cambridge prison rose from his seat, and, producing a number of documents, handed them over to the Queen's counsel. The papers detailed the whole of the particulars of the fifteen burglaries we had committed! John Hart had informed of all!

My rage and despair were unbounded, and it was only by the exercise of an almost superhuman effort that I controlled myself from heaping on the head of the traitor the appalling execrations which quivered on my tongue.

When the jury retired to consider their verdict, I addressed the judge, stating that, as I had been informed that prisoners could transfer their property to any person they chose, I desired to make over the money I possessed to my heartbroken mother. The Government had between £200 and £300 belonging to me, which the police found secreted about me after my arrest. No claim of identification was put in for any portion of this money, and the judge graciously sanctioned the request I made. Luke also requested permission to do likewise, which was granted. The money was shortly afterwards sent to my mother, who had no alternative but to accept it.

The jury returned into court with a verdict of guilty, and the judge, before passing sentence, asked us if we had anything to say in extenuation of our crimes. I at once expressed my indigation at the manner in which our conviction had been brought about, when an acquittal stared us boldly in the face.

His Honour in passing sentence said we were all young men, and in consideration of our youth he would impose upon us a term of fifteen years transportation.

The sentence was comparatively light for the crime with which we were charged at that time, though in these enlightened days it would be deemed a cruel punishment.

But fifteen years transportation appeared to me equal to being consigned to a living grave. What a vista of utter misery and torture stretched before me. Surely death itself would be thrice welcome before the enforcement of such a life.

Heedless of the consequences, as these despairing thoughts rushed through my mind, I showered a tirade of abuse upon the treacherous John Hart, and would there and then have committed some bodily injury upon him had not the warders come to his assistance.

I despised the efforts of my gaolors, however, and used my fists to the best advantage. Law and order were deposed from the hall of justice, and consternation reigned supreme, for those few moments, until I was at length overpowered by force of numbers, and conducted from the dock.

As I grew rational, it was some satisfaction for me to know that John Hart had reaped no benefit by his ignoble action. His confession had been voluntary, and therefore the Crown had used it gratuitously and to the best advantage.

Soon after our sentence we were sent to Milbank prison, the receiving depot for transportation men. John Hart was not drafted away in the company of my brother, myself and Tom Hart, for the authorities apparently still dreaded an outburst of violence from me. We remained at Milbank eight or nine months, during which time we were fairly comfortable. I gradually grew more resigned to my position, and in consideration of my good conduct I was ordered by my superviser (Mr. Finney) to go to the general wards, where the prisoners were employed at tailoring.

The workshop was long and narrow, and contained a row of benches down either side, facing each other.

Strangely enough, I was placed in a vacant seat directly facing John Hart, the very man I should not have been thrown into contact with. When dinner time came, we obtained some license to move about, and I seized the oportunity to accost my late companion in crime.

"John Hart," I said, menacingly, and with a tone of solemnity that I could assume so well, "you have signed your death warrant. You know how determined I am; you know that I am never thwarted in my wishes; and on the first opportunity, I shall surely put an end to your existence and so revenge myself."

My gestures and the inflections of my voice made such an impression on Hart that no sooner had I uttered them than his features grew swollen and discoloured, a spasm twisted his lips, and he fell speechless and motionless to the ground like a man stricken with apoplexy.

He was at once picked up and taken to the hospital, and two or three days afterwards the head chaplain informed me that the unfortunate man was dead, and that it was reported that his death had been brought about by the fright he received from me. I assured the chaplain that it was predestination; John Hart's time had come. I also expressed my regret that he had not died before he obtained our conviction.

The sedentary work I was engaged at was not to my taste, although the prisoners in this ward slept in more desirable quarters and were placed on better diet. After a little time I requested the supervisor to remove me to my former cell, a request which he granted.

While confined here I learned to read and write, and the gentleman who taught me said I was one of the most apt of his pupils. My brother Luke could read and write before his sentence; but, as I have before stated, I had never even learned the alphabet. I made such quick progress under my teacher's guidance, that after a lapse of six months I wrote a letter to my brother William.

Then I became seized with a desire to know something about religion, and I read the commandments over and over again, as well as those portions of the Bible which I could understand.

I was particularly struck with the words—"Remember the Sabbath day to keep it holy. Six days shalt thou labour, and do all that thou hast to do; but the seventh day is the Sabbath of the Lord thy God. In it thou shalt do no manner of work," etc.

"It is not right for me to work on Sundays," I said to myself, and communicated my impression to the superviser.

"You must do as the authorities tell you," said he.

"No," I replied, "I shall do as God tells me.

I was ordered to take a hand at the pump to draw water as usual on the Sunday following this conversation, but I refused to obey.

"It is only a matter of form," the warder (Mr. King) said, but I emphatically declared I would have nothing to do with work on the Lord's day.

"Very well," said Mr. King, "I shall have to report you for insubordination: it is open rebellion before the other prisoners."

"You may do what you please," I said, "but I will not work on Sunday."

"I am very sorry for you," said Mr. King, "for during the time you have been working here, you have done as much as any two of the other prisoners."

On the following morning I was brought before the governor of Milbank, who asked me what I had to say for myself, as if I had done something very wrong.

I told him quietly that I would work well on the week days, but not on Sundays.

"But," said he, "do you not see that by this persistent refusal to obey orders, you incite the other prisoners to rebellion? We must keep order and discipline in the prison."

I was not to be moved by this argument, and so strongly had my devout impressions fastened upon me that I informed the governor I did not want anything to eat on Sundays except food which had not been cooked on that day.

Well, to be brief, I was sentenced to three days in the "black hole" for disobedience of orders.

The superviser, however, spoke on my behalf, for I had always worked hard, and he used his influence to get the punishment revoked, in which he was successful.

I told him, however, that this kindness would not have the least effect on my determination.

"You may hang me to a tree," said I, "but I must and will obey God's commandments."

After that reply I was sent back to my cell again, and two clergymen were sent to me, one of whom (Mr. Penny) took the Bible, and pointed out where the disciples plucked the ears of corn and ate them on the Sabbath day. He explained the reply of Jesus, who held them blameless, and he then endeavored to convince me that there was no harm in pumping water for drinking on the Sabbath day.

"Well, then," I said, "what are the commandments of God for if we are not to obey them?"

The chaplain said they were to be obeyed, but that my spiritual advisers were better able to discriminate right and wrong actions in accordance with them.

In spite of these arguments and persuasions, I still persisted in my refusal, and they left fully convinced that any further attempts to induce me to alter my decision would only prove futile.

It was the rule in the case of transported prisoners to be brought before a Board, who decided upon where they were to be sent to serve their probation, and I prayed that my brother Luke—of whom I was very fond—and I should be removed to the same place to fulfil this term.

This request was sanctioned by the Board, but during the night after this communication was made to me, I was seized with English cholera, and it was feared that the attack would prove fatal I may state that the epidemic was very prevalent among the prisoners at this time, but that they were made as comfortable as possible under the circumstances, receiving half a pint of porter per day, and also special treatment

This illness prevented me from accompanying my brother, who, with Tom Hart, was sent to Wakefield, in Yorkshire, thence to Portland, and ultimately to the Swan River, Western Australia.

As for me, when I had sufficiently recovered from my illness to be removed, I was sent to the hulk Warrior at Woolwich Here we had our meals by day, and slept in classes of fourteen or fifteen by night, the major portion of our time being spent in laborious work in the dockyards

CHAPTER IX

A Miserable Time—Starvation—Inhuman Cooks—A Fight for Justice—The "Black Hole"—Tyranny—Open Rebellion—Desperate Deeds—More "Black Hole" and Irons.

Oh, what a period of misery I went through at Woolwich! It all comes back to my memory as it it had only happened yesterday Starvation, misery, and want beset me on every side Day after day my life was horrible, and I cursed existence

There was a system of swindling carried on at the hulks that my readers will scarcely believe Certain of the prisoners of the better classes—"flash" chaps I called them—who obtained money secretly from their friends, were permitted to purchase extra food, and this was actually deducted from the supplies of the poor unfortunate men who were not in a position to buy, with the result that they were in a state of semi-starvation!

Did I complain? Yes; over and over again But Mr. Masterman ,the captain of the "ship," said I was a big strapping fellow, and always complaining unnecessarily

"Yes," I said, "I am big enough, but my strength will not stand against such low diet I am weak, and shall soon drop dead from starvation!"

I pointed out to him that the meal porridge was too thin, and that we were defrauded of a portion of the substance I told him I could read the regulations, which specified that for a quantity not exceeding 50 pints, two ounces of meal per pint were allowed, and exceeding 50 pints an ounce and a half I assured him that the gruel was not of sufficient substance, and was, as a matter of fact, too poor to sustain us

"Very well," he replied, "I'll give you an ounce and a half of meal and if you don't make a pint of the 'smuggings,' as thick as this (pointing to the watery compound served out to us) I'll put you in cross irons and 'black hole' you."

I remarked that this was an unjust demand, as the regulations permitted two ounces of meal for any quantity under 50 pints. He would not alter the allowance, however, and instructed the steward to give me an ounce and a half of meal, and a quart saucepan to boil it in. The steward complied, and then took me to the officers' galley to try my skill. He strove his utmost to induce me to put salt into the saucepan, but this I refused to do, knowing that it would have the effect of making the porridge thin.

I made the porridge without further interference, and took it to Mr. Masterman, who pronounced it good and thick, and ordered that I should be put into the cookhouse to make the "smiggings," as we used to call it.

But I had an uphill battle to fight against the other cooks, who were afraid of being robbed of the money which they received from the "flash" prisoners, who profited by their purchases, and waxed fat.

To show my readers how we were treated, before I was placed in the cookhouse, I may mention, as an actual fact, that one man dropped dead from starvation!

Now came the big struggle for food!

One Sunday evening I had finished making the gruel, when each of the cooks in the cookhouse poured a bucket of cold water into it, the overseer meanwhile laughing and encouraging them. Looking over the hatchway I yelled out in a voice of thunder—

"Stand to your arms, men We will boil these cooks who would spoil our food!"

My blood was up, and I cared not for consequences. The overseer of the cookhouse I knocked flat, serving one of the cooks in the same manner, whilst the remaining one dodged away from me.

"Aid and assist!" cried the cooks and overseers.

I seized the poker to defend myself, but before I could use it they overpowered me, and thrust me into the "black hole."

On the following morning I was brought before Mr. Masterman.

"What have you to say about this rash act?" he asked me.

"Rash act!" I exclaimed. "Am I to submit to this system of robbery and persecution? I only served the overseer and cook as they deserved, and if I had had time I would have massacred the whole lot who were leagued against me."

"Jeffrey," said he, "that temper of yours will bring you to the gallows. Why did you not come to me and complain? I would have given you redress. You have been unjustly treated, it is true, but you had no right to take the law into your own hands." He then gave me twenty-four hours "black hole," and ordered my dismissal from the cookhouse.

It may be presumed that this punishment would have had the effect of making me more amenable to discipline. However, it did not, for I still complained of the system of robbery which prevailed, and when the head inspector (Captain O'Vowells) made his customary visit I detailed to him our sufferings. But he merely laughed in my face, and I was frequently punished for complaining of being defrauded of my rights.

The arbitrary power of those in authority prevented me from obtaining justice.

"Give me justice!" I demanded.

"Give him more solitary confinement!" replied my persecutors.

And Might prevailed over Right..

In a short time the gang I was in was, put to the work of discharging coals from vessels which put in at Woolwich. This work was performed in three stages. I or another prisoner took them from the ship, and carried them about one hundred yards, then others took them, and so on, until they were deposited in the position assigned to them. The overseer, whose name was Charlie Ellis, was a most humane man, and I shall ever bear him in kindly remembrance. I was still, I may remark, devoutly disposed, and under the influence of Ellis's kindness was gradually relapsing into a state of contentment.

One day, however, the second mate of the hulk Warrior, whose name was Joe Allen, said, "Jeffrey, fall out and stand by" (meaning that he was about to transfer me to another gang).

This order was a surprise to me, and one which was distinctly opposed to my wishes, for, as I have said, I was quite satisfied with Charlie Ellis. The captain of the vesssel we were working on also gave us a pint of porter twice a day and extra food, so that my lot had fallen in pleasant places. I hesitated when I received Allen's command, for I had no wish to obey.

"If you refuse to do as I tell you," stormed Allen, "I'll put you in cross irons and 'black hole' you!"

At that moment I had no desire for further punishment and so reluctantly went into the other gang as ordered.

"Fall in! quick march!" said the sentry.

"Slow march!" I countermanded.

I led the sentry to believe that my dislocated ankle was causing me great pain and that I was unable to walk fast, so that the rest of the gang had to follow my example.

In proceeding to my new sphere of labour, I had to descend a number of steps, where they were building a small schooner. As I reached the bottom I saw a ship's treenail lying on one of the steps, and falling quickly on my face, as if by accident, I seized the tool and concealed it under the pit of my arm, between the vest and shirt.

I then felt determined to resent my last persecution to the bitter end. I was desperate on account of the advantages they had taken of me. Every good feeling that had been awakened in my heart seemed for the moment deadened, and I was fit for any wild scheme of revenge. I had been punished for the crimes that cruel treatment had prompted me to commit; but had those who were placed in authority over me a right to increase my punishment by condemning me to a life of torture? Mingled feelings of rage and despair consumed me, and I experienced nothing but a desire to inflict upon my unjust enemies—for they were enemies—well-merited chastisement. My very soul thirsted for vengeance, and my eyes longed to gaze on these tyrannical masters lying conquered at my feet.

Still I retained some degree of discretion. I knew that it was prohibited by the authorities to fire on a man or bayonet him unless he molested an overseer or attempted to escape, and so I controlled my passion.

"Right about face! Double!" I shouted at length to the bewildered sentry, and before he had recovered his composure I was running back to the hulks, with him after me. Of course he could not shoot, for there was no evidence to show that I wished to escape.

When I reached the hulk, I went forward to the quarter-deck, where offences are tried, and the sentry coming up shortly afterwards, he charged me with insubordination. Of course the sentry was not aware that I had the weapon concealed under my arm.

Mr. Masterton was called from his cabin to hear the offence by one of the officers He took up a position facing me in the bows of the vessel, whilst the second mate took up a position on my left, and the two guards fronted on the right. I mention this, for I had determined to use the weapon I had concealed as soon as an opportunity presented itself. The sentry who had followed me and laid the charge was instructed to go back to his post, as my case would be remanded for further investigation. On going down the landing, however, he was accosted by the first mate, and the two remained at the cabin door in conversation.

"Well, Jeffrey," said Mr. Masterton, "at your old tricks again. Always complaining. What is the trouble this time?"

I told him that I had been removed without just cause or authority from a gang who were receiving porter and extra food during the day, and that I had only received three ounces of meat for dinner instead of five.

You will have to go into the other gang as ordered," he said, "and do without the extra food. You are always making complaints."

"Yes," I replied, "but you never give me any redress. But I will not stand it much longer; I will have justice."

"Guards, take him away to the 'black hole' for further investigation," said Mr. Masterman.

Ere they had advanced towards me to fulfil these instructions, I stooped quickly, crying out that I had been suddenly seized with cramp. With lightning-like rapidity I withdrew the treenail from where I had concealed it, and before they had guessed my purpose I had felled the

second mate to the deck with a sudden blow on the back
of his head. I then made a powerful blow at Mr. Masterman, but the sentry had by this time recovered from his
surprise, and he advanced towards me with fixed bayonet.
To avoid this weapon, I took a pace to the rear in order
to parry it, and the blow was therefore diverted from the
head of Mr. Masterman. The sentry still pressed towards
me at the point of the bayonet, and in order to escape
from him I was compelled to jump to the lower deck.
The sentry followed me, but as I had no desire to injure
him in any way, and as I moreover knew that he had no
great desire to wound me, I cried out—

"Stop; I will give you my weapon, as I cannot injure
those I wish."

I then consented to walk before the guards to a small
place in the yard where the implements for cross-ironing
were kept.

Let me explain that when a man was in cross or checker
irons it was almost impossible for him to move more than
a few inches at a time.

As soon as I entered the building, I saw a block and
knife close by the door. Not satisfied with what I had
already done, I rushed towards the block, and seizing the
knife, hurled it with all my strength at the guards who
followed me. Fortunately, my aim was not true, and the
knife whizzed harmlessly over their heads.

They then threatened to use their "cutlashes" as we
called them (cutlasses), when I submitted to the irons
being put on me by the blacksmith, and after this I was
thrust into the "black hole."

It was aptly termed "black," for it was a place of utter
darkness. What misery I suffered during these periods
of detention I cannot describe. I was cold and hungry
and despairing, but it was impossible for me to govern
my mad temper while I was being harrassed by persecutions on every hand, and many a scheme of revenge did

CHAPTER X.

More Torments—A Bad Night and a Bitter Awakening— An Impostor—More Tricks—Beefsteaks and Onions, and Beer—Newgate—The Hand of Friendship.

For three hours I lay quietly enough in the "black hole," and slept a little, but the torments I endured prevented me from indulging for any length of time in repose.

"If I cannot sleep," I thought, "at least I will prevent others from doing so." I started to my feet, and shouted till I was hoarse, cursing and blaspheming with all the strength of my lungs. What a night I gave them. At last one of my guards came and peered through a hole at me.

"Out of that," I yelled, "or I'll make trouble for you."

Finally I became exhausted, and dropped off to sleep. Then the guards rushed in upon me, and, taking advantage of my condition, placed the body-irons upon me. These irons, I may state, were fastened around the waist, and had partitions in which the hands were secured.

In the morning they gave me no breakfast, but at dinner time they offered me some bread.

"Oh, you treacherous wretches!" I shouted. "How long am I to endure these sufferings? But wait a little while; I'll catch you when you are not aware of it, and then I'll murder the lot of you." And notwithstanding the starvation I had undergone, I felt powerful enough to carry out my threat. "I would have killed you yesterday," I continued, "had not the opportunity failed. When that was done I would have severed your heads from your bodies and made a good job of it!"

My readers will understand the state of my mind when I thus repeat the threats I used. I am not naturally cruel; but I believed that if I fulfilled my threats I would have been doing a good work to rid the world of a set of monsters; for they were not human in any sense of the word, and did not deserve to live, nor were they fit to die. When they threatened to have me hanged, I shouted that I did not care, for I sought death as a release from suffering.

Towards evening, by order of Mr. Masterman, they released me from the body-irons, conditionally on my good behaviour, and gave me some "smiggings" to eat.

On the following morning I was visited by a clergyman.

"Well, Mark," he said, "I will look after you; you will not be hanged.

"Hanged!" I cried. "Do you think I care for hanging? You look after me! Why did you not look after me before?" Then in my mad rage I rushed at him, and, hampered though I was by "checker' irons, I succeeded in pushing him outside.

"Impostor that you are," I shouted; "hypocrite! Don't come near me, or I'll smash every bone in your body! I wish to be hanged, so that I may not live among such a set as you!"

That night I resumed my conduct of the previous evening. No one within hearing could sleep for the discordant noise I made. About midnight Mr. Masterman came to me and said—

"Mark, if you will promise to be quiet, I will let you out of this cell and put you in one with a window in it."

"I will promise nothing," I said, "until you give me something to eat. You would have been a dead man now if it had not been for that sentry. There are four of you whom I wish to kill, you treacherous, inhuman brutes."

He then went away, apparently deeming me hopeless.

Next morning I sent for him again, and he told me the guards could not sleep owing to the noise I made. I promised him that if he sent me a pint of porter I would keep quiet, and this he did.

Shortly afterwards Captain O'Vowells came round.

"Who persuaded you to act in this way?" he asked.

"Wait a moment," I replied. "Did I not make complaints to you on several occasions, and did you not laugh in my face? Have I not been starved and treated like a dog?"

He said he could not give me redress, and he threatened to have me committed and hanged if I did not adopt different tactics.

"Very well," I replied, "you may hang me, but if I get another chance before that time, I will murder some of you, you tyrannical monsters."

I was confined in this cell for some time, and only allowed out occasionally for exercise.

One day, however, the guards wanted me to go back rather soon, and I refused to do so, telling them that I had not had sufficient exercise. They threatened to bring their cutlasses to me, and hearing this, my blood grew hot, and picking up a stone I struck one a severe blow which felled him to the ground.

Mr. Masterman came, and, after hearing my complaint, said I was to have as much exercise as I liked. "We don't want to injure you," he said, and under those conditions I kept quiet.

"Show me some pity and humanity," I said, "and I will give you no further trouble," but Captain O'Vowells gave me to understand that he would have me committed again.

"No he wont," Mr. Masterman replied. But at the same time he had done what he could against me, for a week afterwards the guards came and told me I was to be removed to Wakefield, where my brother Luke was. If I consented to have the body-irons put upon me quietly, they informed me I should have beefsteaks and onions and beer when we reached London.

"But why put me in body-irons?" I asked. "Will not the guards be with me in the omnibus?"

"It is Mr. Masterman's order," they replied.

"Very well," said I, "bring your cutlasses, for if you attempt to put me in body-irons I'll trouble some of you!"

At last Mr. Masterman consented to allow me to have my right hand free from confinement, as I requested, and under those conditions I permitted the guards to once more put the body-irons upon me.

We then set out for London, and now I will tell you how they deceived me by promising me beefsteaks and onions. Instead of being taken to Wakefield, I was taken to Newgate gaol, which I recognised when I saw it. I knew my brother Luke was not there, and I had very poor hopes of beefsteaks and onions.

I therefore turned sharply round, and suddenly struck one of the guards a heavy back-handed blow with my disengaged first.

This created a scene, and a crowd collected, but I was very soon placed in prison.

The governor of Newgate—"Old Cope," we called him —was a most humane man, and a Christian gentleman, whom I shall never forget. He came to me and said:—

"Jeffrey, don't you know that all this resistance to authority is useless, and only makes your punishment more severe? We can call the soldiers, and you will certainly be injured if you persist in such mad behaviour."

Seeing what kind of a man he was, I told him my story —how cruelly I had been treated; how I had been starved and put in the "black hole" merely because I had complained of ill-treatment.

"Well," he said, "we do not allow that sort of thing here. Do you, if any of the officers maltreat you in any way, tell me all about it, and I will see that it does not continue. But I must keep order here, and if you behave in a riotous way you must be punished."

He then showed me a man who was confined in the prison for shooting at the Queen. He was stark naked, and had been behaving like a madman—shouting and smashing everything within his reach.

I was placed in one of the condemned cells, and that night I slept well. In the morning I heard one of the guards call the prisoner who occupied the cell adjoining mine. He used very harsh language towards the man, speaking to him as if he was a dog.

"Oh," thought I, "you just wait, my fine gentleman, and if you put your head inside my cell and speak to me in that manner I'll knock your brains out against the wall!"

Presently he came to me.

"Good morning," he said, looking at me as if I was a curiosity.

"Good morning," I returned, rather sulkily.

"Will you get up and make your bed?" he asked.

I sprang out of bed very willingly at this request, for it pleased me to be spoken to so kindly.

He then entered into conversation with me about Yorkshire, and then he began to admire my stalwart figure and knotted muscles. He had heard, he said, of my last exploit in the dockyard, and appeared to be somewhat awed in my presence He seemed bent on making a friend of me, for he laughingly expressed a hope that I would not knock him about as I had done the others

"Treat me well," I said to him, "and you will be safe, but use me harshly, and I'll wait for a time and then attack you treacherously, and you may as well tell the mates that will relieve you the same thing"

He assured me that he would do so, and before leaving he produced some rum, in a draught of which we mutually pledged our compact

----

CHAPTER XI

Kind Treatment—A Mean Sister—Penal Servitude for Life—Longing to be Hanged!—I Feign Lunacy—Pentonville—Bound for the Antipodes—"A Good Man When Fed Well, but Desperate When Raw!"—The Fruits of Hunger

The following morning a fresh warder came to me, and he treated me in the same conciliatory manner, as, in fact, they all did. But one day, while I was walking in the yard taking my accustomed exercise, the under-governor came up and pompously ordered me back to my cell.

As I had only been out for about an hour, I resented his interference, and emphatically refused to obey him

"I am here awaiting my trial for assault on the second mate of the hulks," I said, "and as it is customary to allow prisoners awaiting their trial to have as much exercise as they desire, I will stay out here all day if I choose to do so"

"Very well," he replied, "I'll bring a body of guards to you and we'll see if you will do as you like."

I rushed at him with the intention of knocking him down with a blow, but he evaded me, and running into the adjoining yard closed the door in my face

By-and-by old Mr Cope came to me and asked for an explanation I told him that the under-governor had ordered me to my cell before I had sufficiently exercised myself He was quite satisfied with my statement, and gave orders that I was to be permitted to have the same privileges as the other men awaiting trial, and be allowed to stay out all day if I desired to do so

About this time I made a request that I should be "taken off the country," as I wished to maintain myself, and not live at the expense of the Government.

Mr Cope would not allow this, however, but told me I should have as much food as was necessary, and at my request allowed me an additional bottle of porter a day so long as I behaved myself

Shortly after this I wrote to my sister Emily, who was

housekeeper for Lady Cotton ,and expressed a wish that she should send me money to pay for my defence. To this she replied in effect that if I had taken care of my money, as she had done, I would not have had any need to apply to her for assistance. In fact, she refused to aid me. I had, she said, been very rash, and she was sorry she had not sent me a Prayer-book and Bible as she had to my brother Luke. To this cheering epistle I replied, calling my sister and also my aunt heartless misers, and assuring them that their money would never do them any good.

I went on very well for a little time, and Mr. Cope appeared to be very much pleased at my behaviour. He was exceedingly kind to me, and even gave me flannels, which he had provided out of his own money, because I had complained of the intense cold. He told me that I should not plead guilty when my trial came on; but I acknowledged my intention of relating to the court how I had tried to "settle four of the wretches," and also detail the circumstances which led me to commit the assault.

In due course I was arraigned for trial, and when the court was in possession of the particulars relative to the assault, I made my statement, which occupied over two hours. I was well-nigh starved, I said, and becoming desperate I made up my mind to kill Mr. Masterman, Allen, and the two guards who were on deck. I did not endeavour to vindicate my action, but, on the other hand, I strove to convince the court that I gloried in the deed and felt no compunction for what I had done. I painted my character in the blackest colours, asserting that I had been driven into this degraded condition by the awful persecution to which I had been subjected. My guilt I freely acknowledged, and besought the judge to pass the sentence my crimes warranted.

The verdict was, of course, "guilty," and the judge sentenced me to penal servitude for life, adding that I was to be sent to Norfolk Island.

This sentence was not in accordance with my wishes, and no sooner had it been pronounced than I addressed this impartial administrator of the law as follows:—

"Your Honour, I have been convicted of attempted murder, and I confess that I would have carried out the deed if I had not been frustrated. Why do you not perform your duty fearlessly, and sentence me to be hanged? Life in gaol is worse than torture to me, and I long for hanging, so as to be removed from such a cowardly, tyrannical mass of humanity as that in authority over the helpless prisoner. I call upon your Honour to carry out the law to its fullest extent. It is your duty to do so, and if I had the means I would shoot you at the present moment and so make sure of what I most desire—the gallows."

I was not allowed to proceed any further after uttering this threat, but was at once hurried back again to durance vile in Newgate by my keepers. One of the warders informed me on the following morning that my speech caused considerable sensation in the court, and that one of the leading papers had published a full account of my case under the heading "Longing to be Hanged!"

Whilst awaiting my removal from Newgate, I was allowed considerable latitude and comfort by Mr. Cope He gave permission for a schoolmaster to visit me for a short time each day, and aided by his guidance I wrote a petition to Sir George Grey, who was then Home Secretary, praying that I should be hanged and put out of my misery I detailed the full circumstances of my case, and pointed out that the judge had departed from his proper course of duty

The second day after the schoolmaster had left me, I felt an inward prompting to feign madness Mechanically I yielded to this strange inspiration, and stripping every particle of clothing off my body I tore it into shreds Then I devoted similar attention to the writing table and my bedding, meanwhile using my powerful voice to the best advantage, and ramping and roaring around my cell like a newly-caged beast

My guards came and peered at me through the eyelet-holes of the cell Apparently my appearance and assumed conduct produced such a terrible effect that they were afraid to enter, content at watching me in silence with awe-stricken eyes, and from a safe vantage point.

Two hours' pursuit of this line of action weakened me considerably, and also threw me into a profuse perspiration I then threw myself on the floor, groaning as if helpless and in terrible pain

This infused courage into my keepers, and shortly afterwards one of them entered, accompanied by a doctor I was now only groaning slightly, as if utterly exhausted, and the doctor bent over me, examining my limbs, and expressing words of sympathy towards me. He prescribed cold fomentations for the head at regular intervals, and instructed them to keep me well covered up

He informed the warder that I was suffering from temporary insanity, which he considered had been brought on by the worry I had undergon in preparing my petition to Sir George Grey

The medical gentleman then took his departure, and the warder began to bathe my head, at the same time uttering words of sympathy Suddenly I jumped to my feet with renewed energy, and gave vent to a deafening roar with the full power of my lungs This so alarmed the warder that he took his departure unceremoniously, but so precipitate was he in his movements that he fell down the stairs leading from the cell and injured two ribs.

Throughout the remainder of the day I continued to rave and roar, and worked myself into such a state that I actually frothed at the mouth

On the following day the doctor, accompanied by two guards, came in upon me unawares I was at once seized and placed in a staight jacket. The doctor then examined me, and asked several questions, to which I made ridiculous and disconnected replies. He gave the warders some instructions concerning my treatment, and hinted that if I was no better on the following day it would be advisable to send me to a lunatic asylum.

I was now guarded by two of the warders, and by the time the doctor visited me next day, I was heartily tired of maintaining the deception. I therefore greeted him most cordially, and laughingly referred to all that had transpired.

But the doctor was a passionate man, and he did not accept my revelation with good grace, as he had been befooled and belittled before all the officers of the gaol.

"I presume, doctor, you have not had much experience in mental diseases?" I queried sarcastically as the straight jacket was being removed from me.

"No insolence, scoundrel!" he exclaimed, angrily, with a stamp of the foot, and he then abruptly left the cell. I ascertained that he reported the affair to the authorities, but no action was taken by them.

Shortly after this incident I was removed to Pentonville, a model prison in London, and had not been long located there before I began to complain of short allowance. I told the doctor that I only received sufficient food to support a child—five ounces of bread for each meal, and half a pound of potatoes, and a morsel of meat each day.

"There is many a man in London who does not get as much as that," he said.

"London!" I exclaimed; "they are all dwarfs there, but I am a man six feet one inch in height and fifteen stone in weight, and it requires more than what I get to support me."

"Do you want any more gruel?" he asked.

"No," I replied. "Do you think I want such stuff as that? Give me some porter and an extra loaf each day."

"Very well," he said, "you will have what you require," a promise he faithfully carried out.

My conduct in this prison was much better, and the governor commended me on more than one occasion, and also wrote to Sir George Grey giving me a good character. My reputation had, however, preceded me, and many of the warders held me in dread.

It was customary for the warders to shave the prisoners belonging to their respective divisions, and to show how easily frightened was the old warder over me, I may relate that on one occasion when he was shaving me the razor was rather rough, and becoming slightly annoyed, I jumped to my feet. He was so terrified that he ran away shouting for help, and in his hurry fell over the doorstep, upon which I picked him up and assured him that I meant no injury.

I was put to making coats in the prison, and one day the master tailor came to me and said—

"How many coats have you made?"

"Never mind," I replied, "I don't intend to give them to you, I want them for a bed to lie on during the day. Don't worry me too much or I'll 'do' for you"

The master tailor did not trouble me much about the work after that, and I did not do much tailoring.

In the course of time I learned from a Scotch doctor named Anderson, during a conversation in the cell, that I was to be sent to Australia, in the ship Eliza, with a number of other desperate prisoners, and in a month after that time we were escorted to where that vessel was lying at Woolwich. A number of omnibuses had been secured and partitioned off, so that the prisoners were not thrown into contact with each other, and there was no risk of danger arising on the journey There were sixty of us, and we were all termed incorrigibles, so that some precautionary measures were extremely necessary.

On the way to Woolwich several of the prisoners broke the partitions and created a mild scene; but we were at length placed safely aboard and sent below.

We were divided into four classes of fifteen each, and separated by strong partitions, to prevent us from concocting any plan to mutiny.

When we got to sea, however, the Scotch doctor to whom I have previously alluded gave instructions for these partitions to be removed He did not fear us, he said, and there was no danger of mutiny He carried his fearlessness so far, in fact, that he had his hammock swung near us, and slept in our midst on many occasions. We became extremely attached to him, and every man respected his friendship and the confidence he had reposed in us

The inevitable trouble about my food came in due course. It may appear strange that there should have been so many complaints on my part in this particular direction, but my bodily constitution was so vigorous as to necessitate a somewhat proportionate amount of food I could not withstand the gnawing pangs of hunger, and would have committed any rash act to appease them To substantiate this, I may refer to the police record, which stated "A good man when well fed, but desperate when raw!"

Doctor Anderson was very indulgent towards me, and gave me additional wine every day Whatever I wanted, he said I was to have I was allowed a quantity of flour, and I used to pound up my biscuits and mix them with the flour for the purpose of making puddings, of which I was very fond

On one occasion when my back was turned two or three of the prisoners combined, and took my pudding from the galley I was quick enough to catch them, however, and, whipping up one of the belaying pins from the side of the vessel I hurled it at them with all the force at my command It must have killed one if my aim had been true, but fortunately it was not. The doctor when he came for an explanation told me I could have double allowance on the following day, but this would not suit me, and he at length ordered a good dinner to be sent to me, and I had my fill.

I grew very fond of a prisoner named Josh Edmundson, who, I heard, was afterwards hanged for being concerned in the murder of John Price, the commandant of Norfolk Island. He was a good singer and dancer, amusements which I could both enjoy and participate in myself.

One night it was agreed that the soldiers and the prisoners should have a singing match, and while engaged in this pleasant way of passing the tedious hours, Edmundson suggested that we should filch some pork. He knew where there were some barrels of it, he said, and could easily obtain it. I remonstrated with him, and emphatically refused to have anything to do with the proposal. I had not, however, been in my bunk more than an hour before he came to me with several pieces of pork, about 4lb. each.

"Plant them," he said; "you have a spare corner."

I at first refused; but he pressed me so hard that I at last consented, and subsequently the meat was cooked and eaten. The theft was not discovered, fortunately for us.

A week after this event two men named Proctor and Jerry Galvin killed a sheep and dresed it, and it was cut up for the purpose of making pies. I had nothing to do with it, for I always had sufficient to eat, and I was not desirous to add to my trouble.

CHAPTER XII.

Hobart Town—Norfolk Island—Mr. Montgomery—"The Races"—"Pine-Tree Jack"—A Bad Beating—"Too 'Belly Proud' "—In Irons—Biting a Girl's Nose Off —Orange Vale—Bad Temper and Its Results.

Nothing of moment occurred on the voyage of the ship Eliza between England and Hobart Town. We had an unusually protracted voyage, however, which was chiefly owing to the stormy weather we encountered.

We arrived at Hobart Town in 1850, when Sir William Denison was governor. From our anchorage I gazed upon the savage grandeur of Van Dieman's Land with bitter disappointment. It seemed hard to be banished for ever from the busy hum and gaieties of the old world; to be so utterly estranged from cherished scenes and associations. I had no eye for the picturesque or beautiful; no desire for sylvan glades or health-giving breezes.

"Here is a pretty place to send a man to!" I exclaimed

"I would rather be dead than be compelled to live in a savage country like this!"

To my unbounded satisfaction, it was pointed out to me that I was not to remain there, and in about a week we weighed anchor and sailed for Norfolk Island.

The natural outline of my future home was more in conformity with my taste, for the tropical isle shone out in the rays of the sun like an earthly paradise. The sumptuous colours and glow of the rich foliage of the tropics dazzled the eye, and the colours of fragrant blossoms were delightful.

We were landed at a place called the Cascades, and were met by the commandant (Mr. John Price) and a number of constables.

Our first night was spent at the barracks, and in the morning we had a dish of hominy for breakfast. I had no relish for this kind of diet, but had to rest contented. While we remained at the barracks I was constantly grumbling at the dinner served out to us. The commandant said we were lucky, and pointed to the "sweet bucks," as they called the potatoes. Dr. Anderson also laughed at my complaint, and told me I was fortunate.

The doctor came to us shortly after this, and bade us all good-bye. He told me he had given all of us good characters to the commandant, and had especially referred to me.

On the Sunday after the doctor left, Mr. Belstead (the muster-master) ordered me to go to the house of a Mr. Montgomery (police clerk at that time), which was situated some distance from the barracks, and where I was to serve as gardener.

Mr. Montgomery appeared pleased when he saw me, and sent me into the kitchen for dripstone water, as his two servants had been locked up for getting drunk. He and some of his friends were in the parlour sampling some of the brandy that had arrived by the Eliza.

I went to the kitchen as directed, and my eye fell upon some chilis that were lying on the table. Considering they were a delicacy, I put two or three in my mouth and ate them. They were fearfully hot, and I cried with pain. To show how kind Mr. Montgomery was I may mention that he came to me and did what he could to relieve me, leaving me half-a-pint of brandy.

A few minutes after he informed me that he was going out for a few hours, and he instructed me to take charge of the house, fasten the doors allow no one on the premises, and get his tea ready, at the same time adding that if I did not fulfill these instructions I would be flogged and put in the quarry gang.

Between nine and ten o'clock that night I heard some one on the verandah, and on opening the door found my master there fast asleep.

I awakened him, and told him his tea had been waiting since six o'clock. He did not want anything to eat, however, but _____ _____ ers that I was to tell the commandant's constable, at Government House, to call him early in the morning, for he wanted to go to the races.

"What races?" I asked. "I have not seen any horses except your own horse Cuffy."

"Do as I instruct you," he replied, laughingly. "There will be plenty of horses.

I obeyed him, and after I had delivered the message, I asked the commandant's constable to give me the names of the racehorses.

"Oh," he replied, " you will know all about them to-morrow."

When Mr. Montgomery returned in the evening, I again asked him about the races.

"What horses won?" said I.

"None," he answered. .

"Nonsense!" I exclaimed; "some horses must have won."

I began to get irritated at the evasive replies he made, and seeing this he enlightened me by stating that every Monday morning about 150 incorrigibles were brought up for trial. Some of these were flogged, some spread-eagled and gagged, and others sentenced to solitary confinement.

A few months passed away, during which time I managed to give my master satisfaction. He was a capital fellow, and never desired to see any man punished unnecessarily; but of course he was powerless when they fell into the hands of the police.

The garden at Orange Vale progressed very well under my care, and one day Mr. Montgomery informed me that if I continued in the way I was going, my term of probation would be reduced from two and a half years to twenty months, and that I would become a pass-holder, and be entitled to receive wages amounting to £9 per year.

Our cook, whose name was Joe Case, was a very sociable sort of fellow, and as he always treated me well, I conceived a great liking for him. One day a carter brought a load of wood, and Case said he would give the man something to eat. This, however, was against the regulations, and I told him so.

There was a policeman on the island whom we called "Pine-Tree Jack," owing to a practice he had of spying our actions from the branches of the pine trees, and I knew him to be in the vicinity at the time the carter arrived.

Case, however, said he cared nothing about "Pine-Tree Jack," and soon fried the man some meat, which he set before him.

He had no sooner eaten it, however, than down came "Pine-Tree Jack" and arrested Case, who, for this offence, was sentenced to nine months in the quarry gang.

A man named Joseph Harvey was then engaged by Mr. Montgomery as cook, and before many days had elapsed I foresaw that there would be trouble between us. I worked hard and wanted plenty to eat, but this man placed me on short allowance   I complained to Mr Montgomery about it, and he gave orders that I should have what I required   These instructions, however, were not fulfilled, for the cook gave me bread and tea for breakfast ,and in other ways annoyed me

I bore with him for a time, but one night when I returned from work, I saw that he had placed bread and tea before me, whereas, being ill with dysentery, I had requested him to prepare me some arrowroot   My temper was aroused

"I told you," I said, that I wanted arrowroot, and this is how you obey my wishes"

He replied that he would give me just what he pleased, and placing himself in a fighting attitude he called me a "varmint!"

This irritated me beyond endurance, and I struck him a blow on the cheek, which made the blood flow copiously   The force of it felled him to the floor, and he lay there for a moment motionless

"Get up!" I said, but he refused   He was afraid of me, I could see, so I determined to punish him severely for his impertinence.   I thrashed him unmercifully and almost choked him

"I know I will get nine months for this night's work," I said, "and so I will give you something that will be worth reporting"

I will not describe how I beat him, but I did not stop until he was almost unable to move, and I then said—

"Now you can make your report"

"No," he replied, "I will not do that   I will say, if I am asked, a piece of wood hurt me while we were chopping wood"

"Come with me to the commandant's," I said, "and make your report to the constable on duty   I will go with you"

But he would not do this, and persisted in his determination

On the following morning he informed me that Mr Montgomery wanted me to take his horse, Cuffy, to Long Ridge, two or three miles from the settlement, and get him shod at the blacksmith's shop, but on asking him if the master had given him a written order he said it was not necessary that I should have one

My suspicions at once became excited, because his manner was strange.   I believed that, notwithstanding his assurance to the contrary, he had told his story to Mr Montgomery   Then I shouted out that I would pay him for his treachery, and rushed towards him   At this he ran off, calling "murder!" upon which Mr Montgomery put in an appearance

"What is all this about?" he asked

I informed him of the whole matter, and to my surprise he told me that Harvey had related a very different story, to the effect that because my supper was not quite ready I had beaten him until he was covered with bruises

When I had related my version of the disturbance, Mr. Montgomery said—

"You are both my servants, and I do not wish you to be punished for this affair, but really it is so serious that I must report it to the commandant."

On the following "race day," therefore, I was brought before Mr. Price on a charge of assault, and Harvey gave evidence against me, which was false in every particular.

"What have you to say to this," asked Mr. Price.

"He has told you a tissue of lies," I replied. "I was ill with dysentery and wanted arrowroot, and instead of making it for me he gave me dry bread and tea. Then, because I complained, he called me a 'varmint,' placed himself in fighting attitude, and threatened to knock my head off, whereupon I felled him to the ground."

"You and I will have to fight if you don't mind," said Mr. Price.

"Fight!" I exclaimed. "I will fight any man on the island!"

"Oh, my joker!" he returned; "I will fight you in a very different way—with the cat-o'-nine tails. You are too fresh and strong, too 'belly proud, 'and we must take a little of that out of you."

"That would be cowardly work!" I cried.

"Well," said the commandant, "Mr. Montgomery has given you a good character, and I shall take that into consideration, and give you a week in light irons.

"I am much obliged to you, sir, for your leniency," I said, and away I went.

On reaching the house Harvey wanted to fix the pads—which prevent the irons from chafing—on my ankles, but I would not give him satisfaction, and put the pads on myself.

My master now gave orders that I should have such necessary food as I desired. These instructions were fulfilled, and things went on very well for a time.

I, however, still harboured a craving to be revenged upon Harvey, but "Pine-Tree Jack" placed him beyond my reach. "Pine Tree" had concealed himself on the beams of the house, and detected Harvey secreting tea, sugar, and butter for the baker under the flour he had to take to the bakehouse.

The consequence was that my enemy was arrested, and he received, to my intense gratification, a sentence of nine months in the quarry gang, with heavy irons.

The next cook was a smart scholarly fellow named Ben Minns. I asked him, soon after his arrival, for what crime he had been transported, but for some time he would not tell me. At length, after much persuasion, he complied with my request.

"I was in love with a young girl,' he said, "and she led me to believe that my passion was reciprocated. I found, however, that she was deceiving me, and receiving the attentions of another admirer.. This inspired me to commit the act for which I was sent here. Filled with burning jealousy, I asked her to meet me for the last time, and bid me farewell She consented, and one night we met by appointment After some conversation, I asked her to allow me to kiss her 'It will be our last embrace,' I said She did not decline, and taking her in my arms I drew her to me, but instead of kissing her I seized her nose in my teeth, bit it off, and spat it in her face. 'Now go to your sweetheart,' I said, 'and see if he covets you without a nose!' For this offence I was convicted and sentenced to Norfolk Island for four years."

I quite approved of this peculiar though cruel method of punishing the girl's infidelity, and we became fast friends

I continued to work at Orange Vale garden, and Mr Montgomery obtained the services of a prisoner to assist in the garden, a poor unfortunate fellow who had just completed a sentence of nine months in the quarry gang He was utterly useless to me, but I took compassion on him and put him at work wheeling the manure. Even this he could not do to my satisfaction, and I threatened to get rid of him

"Don't send me back to that quarry gang," he implored, and I could not find it in my heart to refuse his appeal.

We got our supplies of tea and sugar every Saturday night from Mr Montgomery's house, and on one occasion in the middle of the week when I asked for more he said we were using a great deal This irritated me, and I, as usual, lost my temper

"You don't suppose we are selling it!" I exclaimed.

"No," replied Mr Montgomery, "I do not wish to accuse you of doing anything of the kind" He then endeavoured to soothe me, but in my ungovernable rage I refused to listen to him

"Have I not given you proof of my honesty?" I asked

He told me that he was quite satisfied, but I was not, and in my folly I refused to listen to him, saying I would not work for him any longer

"Very well, Jeffrey," he remarked at length "If you are in the same mood to-morrow I will let you go, and will get you another place"

"It may seem strange that I should have allowed such a trifle to separate me from so estimable a master, but so it was I was unforgiving, and the slightest word at that time was sufficient to fill my breast with relentlessness.

On the following morning Mr Montgomery asked me if I had decided to leave him

"Yes," I replied, "I am sulky."

"Mark," he said kindly, "that temper of yours will be getting you into serious trouble yet I pity you, and would not like to part with you, for you are a good servant Why not stop with me and let this trifling matter end here? or if you do not wish to remain, let me get you another master"

"No," I said, "I will not I would not have come to you had you not borne such an excellent name"

"But," he urged, "I would not like to see you put into

the gang, for there you will surely suffer. You will be flogged and put in irons."

"Let them meddle with me," I replied, "and (using a favourite threat of mine) I'll knock their heads off!"

He thought for a moment, and then said the best thing he could do for me was to make me a sub-constable.

"You will get wheaten rations instead of corncracker," he added, "and plenty of tea and sugar instead of hominy."

I consented to this arrangement, and the commandant permitted the appointment to be made. A suit of clothes was procured for me, and I was placed on duty in the lumber yard with another constable.

CHAPTER XIII.

An Altercation—Removal—A False Charge—Dismissal from the Police—Solitary Confinement—Jealousy—"Old Yorkey"—A Villain Unmasked—An Unsettled Period.

I had not been long in the position of sub-constable before trouble came upon me. One morning a load of water was brought into the yard, and the prisoners were engaged to empty it. One was staitoned at the top, dipping the water from the cask and handing the buckets to a man standing below. A quarrel took place between these men, in consequence of one of them spilling water on the other and dropping the bucket on his head. The petty constable ordered me to arrest them and lock them up, but this I refused to do.

"It was a mere accident," I said, "and I am not going to interfere with them."

"I order you to lock those men up," he shouted, and, as I again refused, he reported me to the senior constable, who threatened that he would have me discharged from the police.

I told him he had not that poerw, for Mr. Montgomery and the commandant were my friends.

He succeeded, however, in having me shifted to Longridge, a station some distance from the settlement. I was put on night duty in this new position, my duties being to assist the head constable in the charge of a number of men who were in the dormitories.

An old pensioner, named Sam Wild, who came out with us, was overseer, having been appointed to that position for his vigilance. At certain hours during the night he would come round to see that all was right, and on one occasion, when I had been suffering from dysentery—a complaint that was very prevalent in the place—he put my name on the charge sheet for having been asleep. This was false, for I had been merely sitting down with my head and body bent forward, that being the position in which I suffered less pain.

Two or three nights after this incident, however, a petty constable named Sam Cox, who was in charge with me, fell asleep while sitting on a ladder near the door. Presently the senior constable came in with old "Yorkey," another petty constable. Seeing them approach, I knew that Cox would be punished if caught, and I endeavoured to wake him.

The senior constable detected me in the act, and he shouted out—

"Hold hard, my man! if you wake him up I will get you a sentence."

I immediately shut the entrance door and Sam Cox came up. He swore hard and fast that he had not been asleep, but it was of no avail.

In due time we were brought before the commandant on a charge of sleeping whilst on duty—a very serious offence. I was innocent, as I have pointed out, but Sam Wild swore that he had found me asleep, and as I had no witnesses, and no point whereby I could throw discredit on his evidence, Price found me guilty.

Cox received a sentence of twenty-seven days solitary confinement, and was also fined a sum of money, whilst I was dismissed from the police force, and sentenced to ten days solitary, on a pound of corncracker a day.

This was a terrible punishment for me. I was placed in a cell under the kitchen, and I cursed and swore vehemently when I heard the frying-pan going.

When the ten days had elapsed I was put into the stables to assist in looking after the horses. One of the animals, named Doctor, had been transported from Sydney for fractious conduct. He was very tricky, and fond of biting, but as I had been accustomed to horses at my father's place, I soon tamed him, and after a time he was so quiet that I frequently drove him out when Mrs. Walker (wife of the superintendent of the station) desired me to do so.

This lady and her family were very partial to me, and the prisoner-overseer grew jealous. He said that when taking Mrs. Walker for a drive I used to tell her "yarns."

I did not wish to quarrel with the man, but he still continued his annoyance. One day, however, during my absence, he and another prisoner who was employed in the stable concocted a charge against me, for which I would have received a severe sentence in the event of having been found guilty.

Fortunately, however, the petty constable, named "Yorkey," who had a habit of slinking stealthily about and listening to the conversation carried on between the prisoners, was at the back of the stable at the time the conspiracy was going on, and he heard the prisoner-overseer who was the prime mover in the plot, say that he would get me six months.

When the charge was laid "Yorkey" related to the commandant what he had heard and thus proved my innocence. The result was that the prisoner-overseer himself received an additional six months to his sentence, and I was apponted his successor.

I lived very comfortably in this position; but not for long, however, for my evil genius still pursued me. The superintendent of agriculture said something to me one day which I did not like, and in a fit of temper I threatened him. I was then dismissed from my post and sentenced to fourten days solitary confinement.

At the expiration of that term, I was ordered to go from Longridge to the settlement, to the house of an overseer of a bush gang, named Aaron Price, and act as his gardener. When I reached my destination, I found that Mr. Price was not at home, and his wife, after giving me my dinner, ordered me to feed the pigs.

"The swill bucket is over there," she said, pointing it out to me.

I picked it up, and finding no handle on it I asked her where it was.

"There is no handle," she replied. "You can put it on your head as 'Swabby' does."

"Not this child," said I. "'Swabby' might have done that, but Mark will not. Put it on your own head; it will make your hair grow."

She grew annoyed at my reply, and she said that if I did not do as ordered I would not get any pork.

This only had the effect of making me still more insolent, for I had a great aversion to pork. I then left her and went down the Dam Road. I had not proceeded far when I saw a bull in the Dam Road lane, near a garden, and, prompted by the spirit of mischief, I pulled a couple of panels of the fence off and drove the beast into Mr. Price's field of sweet bucks. Then I sat down and awaited results.

Not long afterwards I perceived "Swabby," the servant to whom Mrs. Price had alluded, approaching with a loaded wheelbarrow. I shouted out to him that I was in great pain and probably dying.

"Swabby," after emptying the load, made a bed for me and assisted me into the barrow (I pretending all the time to be suffering great agony) and wheeled me to the hospital.

Dr. Everett was called, and I told him that I had sprained myself in the groin while trying to drive a bull out of Mr. Price's garden.

The doctor examined the groin, and as there was a swelling there which had originated from a former complaint, my statement was believed. I was at once admitted into the hospital ward, and treated very kindly, as if I had been really ill. After a few days I allowed myself to get better, and was then sent out to cook for a gang of men in the bush, at which employment I for some time gave the overseer and all the men great satisfaction.

Trouble, however, still followed in my train, for one day a cantankerous prisoner who was working in the gang grumbled and found fault with the cooking. The overseer and the other men raised no objection whatever to

the food, and also pronounced that of the malcontent as
being good and properly cooked.

My temper was irritated to such an extent by this little
incident that I there and then severed my connection with
the bush gang.

I was next placed in a gang on the settlement who were
engaged in various descriptions of laborious work; but
shortly afterwards, for an assault I committed on one of
the prisoners, I was sentenced to the quarry gang.

CHAPTER XIV.

The Chain Gang—Bad Water—John Price and Fair Play
—Fifty Lashes—A Brutal Flagellator—Horrible Pun-
ishment—On the Borders of Death—Spies—Martin
Cash.

Doubtless many of my readers will be surprised when
they read of the constantly-recurring punishments I
underwent, and wonder why I made no earnest effort to
shake off the thraldom of my unruly temper and keep it
in subjection. But it is difficult in these enlightened days
to picture the abject misery into which the prisoners were
thrown; to imagine the humiliation, indignities, and persecutions which were heaped upon us; and then to conceive how utterly abased must have been a man's nature
to have borne the burden and heat of the battle with
meekness and resignation. Though my passionate pro-
tests had dragged me into the vilest cells and placed me
on the very brink of the gallows, still time and experience
proved the inefficacy of punishment to humble my proud
spirit. My heart sickened and my senses revolted at the
inhuman tyranny which surrounded us on every side, and
I was ever ready to uphold the just rights I possessed as
a human being; and to protest—by forcible measures, if
necessary—against the persecutions of my gaolers and
keepers with all the indignation of an outraged man.

My transfer to the quarry gang was not likely to have
a wholesome effect upon me. I was forced to roll very
heavy stones, and, with 36lbs. of iron attached to me, I
found my change of condition very much worse than I
had supposed. Then the overseer continually grumbled;
he was never satisfied with my work, and I did not have
the discretion to hold my tongue.

On one occasion when he was bullying me, I called him
a cruel monster, not fit to live, and told him that I would
take the first opportunity that presented itself to "do" for
him.

For this threat I was condemned to more solitary.

I will here relate an incident which will help my readers
to form a faint idea of the character of John Price, the
commandant.

I have already stated that when I could bring a point
in my favour he would invariably give me the benefit of

it. He was tyrannical, it is true; but he was, to a certain extent, fair and impartial. He never swerved from this course of tyranny—a hard, cruel system carried out to the bitter end.

While I was undergoing this last sentence of solitary confinement an overseer used to bring me water to drink, but it was so filthy that I could not touch it until severe thirst compelled me to do so. It was absolutely stinking, and when the commandant came round I informed him of it. He made a thorough investigation into the matter, and found that the water was as I had described it. The casks were filthy, and the liquid they contained horrible. The overseer was severely reprimanded for neglect of duty; but he still continued after this to persecute me.

After this sentence of solitary confinement was terminated I was sent back to the chain gang again, and the overseer resumed his ill-treatment. I determined to murder him when an opportunity presented itself, for I thought my life was a greater misery than ever to me, and I had no desire to live and bear the unmanly cruelties of this wretch. I was in a state bordering on frenzy, and one day when he had irritated me beyond endurance I seized a spade and rushed towards him with the full intention of splitting his head open. But I was heavily ironed, and he therefore had no difficulty in getting out of my way.

Of course, for this offence I was once more brought under the notice of the commandant.

"I will take all the flashness out of you, my joker!" said Price, and he then ordered that I should receive fifty lashes.

A prisoner named Perkinson was the flagellator at this time, and, fortunately for me, he regarded his involuntary duties with the greatest abhorrence; so much so, in fact, that under his hands I escaped with scarcely an abrasion of the skin.

I have seen other prisoners with their backs like raw beef, and when a man came from the hands of Chapman, an expert with the cat, even John Price was satisfied with the severity of the punishment inflicted. Chapman took a special pride in his work, and used to strike so that each blow would make a fresh cut. He met with a fitting end, however, for he was hanged some years after in Launceston for attempting to murder his master. The prisoners liked Perkinson, who was chosen to flog because he had been in the army.

When my flogging was completed, I was put in fifty six pound irons and manacles, in which it was almost impossible for a man to move, and then placed in a refractory cell.

I was now suffering indescribable misery, being unable to rest in any position owing to the torture I was undergoing.

Each day I grew weaker and weaker. The only relief I got was when I was permitted an hour's liberty to eat the accursed mixture called corncracker and to wash myself.

The commandant used to visit me two or three times a week, and, foppishly putting his eyeglass to his eye, regard me with contemptuous insolence.

"How do you like it by this time, big Mark?" he would say.

I never replied, but to show my unquenchable hatred and defiance, spat at him.

After six weeks of this excruciating misery, when I was reduced to a mere skeleton, Price came to me once more, and said—

"How do you like it now, my joker? I think I have taken all the flashness out of you!"

Then I found my tongue.

"You unnatural monster!" I shouted. "What pleasure can it give you to witness the sufferings of your fellowmen? Come, take my place, and learn from experience how a man can enjoy such punishment."

"What!" he exclaimed, "'Belly proud' still! You are strong yet, my joker? I must see if I cannot take it out of you."

He then left me once more to reflection and solitude.

My condition gradually became more and more serious, and a few days after the interview I have just narrated I was to all appearance a dying man.

It will be understood how this change was brought about when I state that I had been existing for nearly seven weeks on a pound of corncracker a day, and this low diet, together with the dysentery which it caused, left me almost without strength. Then for three days I ate nothing at all, and so the seventh week passed.

I remember one little fellow named Fred Spencer, who suffered ninety days of the cruel torture, but it nearly killed him, and it was not until Price saw that further punishment would result in death that he ordered his release. Another prisoner, named Tommy Dutton, was too proud to ask for mercy, until he had been in irons and solitary confinement, with the eternal corncracker, for sixty days, and he also was apparently dying when placed under the doctor's care.

Perceiving that although my spirit was unbroken, my condition was growing serious, the commandant put me in "trumpeter" irons, which were not so severe as those I had worn for seven weeks.

A few days later, however, I found the end approaching. With what little strength I had, I crawled to the door, and by feeble efforts succeeded in attracting the attention of the dispenser, a prisoner named Donney, part of whose duty it was to disect the bodies of the dead.

"Water!" I gasped. "Give me a drink of water, for God's sake, for I am dying!"

Heartless wretch! Though my equal in crime, he laughed in my face, and with a coarse oath turned his back upon me.

Despair seized me; I fell backwards, and hemorrhage ensued.

One of the officers, noticing my condition, sent for Dr. Everett, who expressed the opinion that I would not live twenty-four hours, and on his own responsibility ordered my release from the irons and removal to the hospital.

There I lay for three months, and was treated with considerable kindness. My vigorous constitution again befriended me, and much to the surprise of the doctor I recovered my health, and, being well fed, I grew fat and as strong as ever.

After leaving the hospital I was made warder in the lumber yard, but I soon had to re-enter the hospital, as repeated attacks of dysentery made me so weak that I had to undergo hot fomentations, turpentine being also rubbed into my skin.

The prisoners suffered considerably from attacks of this nature, for dysentery is extremely prevalent in all the tropical islands of the South Seas.

When I was again discharged I returned to my duties in the lumber yard.

A most detestable system of espionage prevailed on the island. Every prisoner who was not manly enough to refuse was called upon to act as spy upon his neighbour Even the commandant had a habit of giving the men tobacco, and afterwards putting the constable on watch to see if they used it; if they did, they were flogged! When men, too, consented to give him information about their fellow-prisoners he would glean all he wanted and then turn round upon them; treatment which they thoroughly deserved. It was impossible, however, for a prisoner under Price's rule to remain long out of trouble.

Martin Cash—whose life a great many people in Tasmania have read with interest—was one of those who gave information concerning his fellow-prisoners. When I was warder in the lumber yard he often came in from the plaiter's shop, where he was overseer, in order to give information to the petty constable, which was surely followed by severe punishment.

My curiosity being aroused by the frequent visits he made, I asked one of the constables, with whom I was familiar, the nature of Cash's business, and he informed me to the effect I have just mentioned.

"What!" I said, "is this the man who is called the 'good bushranger from Van Dieman's Land?'"

The next time I spoke to Martin Cash I accused him of being a coward.

"It is very well for you to say," I observed to him, "that you always treated women kindly, but that was only done to save your own neck."

Martin did not forget to inform the authorities of my language, but they took no action in the matter.

I maintained my position as warder in the lumber yard for some time, and I used to torment the cowardly scoundrels who had "put their fellow-men away." I never stooped to that meanness myself; in fact, as I told the commandant, if I had done so, I would not have received so many sentences for solitary confinement.

"You'll never die a natural death!" I said to **Price** on one occasion; "there is a curse upon you, for you have no heart. But some day, when you are not aware of it, I will take you treacherously, and have your life. It would be charity to rid the world of a monster such as you!"

As before stated, it was impossible, under this man's rule, to remain long at rest. One man would get "solitary" for chewing tobacco, another for an offence of an equally trivial nature. Every "race day" about one hundred men, and sometimes many more, would be brought up for punishment, and ordered to be either flogged, spread-eagled and gagged, or some other punishment inconsistent with lawful rule.

I will admit, however, that many of the miseries I suffered were the fruits of my own passionate temper and stubborn nature, for had I remained in the service of Mr. Montgomery I would have enjoyed a comparatively happy existence on Norfolk Island. Successive punishments failed to produce any effect upon me, and I continued to struggle openly and firmly for my just rights and against persecution until the end.

CHAPTER XV.

Norfolk Island Abandoned—Port Arthur—I Become a Passholder—A New Master—Mahogany Beef—A Fatal Shot—Dissatisfaction—A Successful Threat.

The settlement at Norfolk Island was broken up in, or about, 1853, and we were then removed to Port Arthur. We were all placed together on the passage thither, there being no classification whatever.

Some of the prisoners were called "blue marks," an opprobrious name, indicating that they had acted as John Price's spies and informers.

We had an awful time in the ship during the passage. There were continual rows and fights.

A prisoner called "Dubbo," who had suffered a great deal at Norfolk Island in consequence of these "blue marks," struck one of them, a prominent ringleader named Proctor, a very heavy blow on the head with a bottle he had concealed, and cut him severely.

The horrors of that voyage I shall never forget, for it was an unbroken period of fighting, shouting and swearing.

When we arrived at Port Arthur, I was put into what was called the farm gang. My strength and dexterity were soon observed by the overseer, who complimented me on my knowledge of the work, and promised to secure a good situation for me. I informed him that I had been accustomed to work at gardening for my father in England, and that we invariably produced the biggest and best crops in Newmarket. He then sent me to the residence of a chaplain, who was in need of a good gardener, but on waiting on the reverend gentlemen he said I was not the man he wanted. I told him that I had no particular desire to enter his employ, as I was well off and satisfied with my treatment in the farm gang. Being on the point of leaving the house, he ran after me and induced me to go back, after which he took me into the grounds and asked me how much manure a grass paddock attached to the house would take. He appeared pleased with my answer, and grew familiar with me. We had a glass of grog together, over which he prevailed upon me to stay.

After I had been in his employment for a few days and given entire satisfaction he proposed to give me ten per cent. on the produce of the farm, in order to encourage me to put forth my best efforts. This was about the time of the Victorian goldfields rush, and potatoes were fetching £20 per ton and onions £30.

I willingly accepted the offer, and also made two or three hundredweight of jam, which we sold for two shillings per pound, so that my perquisites were considerable.

One day my master came to me with the good news that the term life prisoners had to serve to obtain a ticket-of-leave had been reduced from twelve to six years.

A short time after this I was forwarded from Port Arthur to Hobart Town gaol as a passholder, in order to finish my probation for a ticket-of-leave, the time having nearly expired.

I had, however, only been in gaol a short time when I was assigned out as a passholder to a Mr. ——, at the Sandspit, twelve miles from Spring Bay.

On my way thither I learned that Mr. —— was a master who was in the habit of punishing his servants very severely for the least offence. He was a justice of the peace, who had great influence with the Comptroller-General, and very frequently his servants were sentenced to three years 'imprisonment. Upon hearing this I made up my mind that he should not take advantage of me, and that if he tried to do so I would discover some method of curing him.

It was between nine and ten o'clock in the evening when I arrived at my destination, as I lost my way in the bush. I informed my master that I had been sent from the Hobart Town Barracks to work for him as a milkman and gardener, whereupon he looked at me from head to foot with a piercing eyes, as if taking mental observation of my character and abilities. He then instructed another manservant to take me into the kitchen and tell the servant girls to give me some supper, after which I was to be shown to No. 2 hut and sleep there.

But I found that the rest I so much needed was not easily obtained. The hut swarmed with bugs, and they attacked me from every side, until I felt considerably irritated at having been put into such a filthy place, and I resolved that if my master did not provide more suitable accommodation for me he would suffer in some way at my hands.

I was astir early on the following morning and awaiting instructions, when my master beckoned me into the store-room to remove a cask of salt beef. I pulled it on its edge and with a skilful movement placed it in its new position.

Instantly the feat was performed my master threw his hat on the floor and jumped on it, a way he had, I was subsequently informed, of signifying his pleasure.

"You're the man for me!" he shouted boisterously.

After I had done one or two things to his entire satisfaction, he told me that he did not want a milkman and gardener, but there were two or three acres of carrots I could single out and attend to according to my own judgment.

I commenced on this work, and during the day my master came and watched me for a time, expressing his astonishment at the amount of work I had done. He was, in fact, so profuse in his commendations that he told his wife in the evening that I was "the most wonderful man" he ever had on the farm.

That evening the bugs were worse than ever, and I resolved to seek a change. In the morning I waited on Mr. ———, and asked him how I suited.

"Very well indeed, Mark," he replied heartily.

"Then," I rejoined, "your place does not suit me. If you wish to retain my services, you will have to provide me more suitable accommodation. Your garden hut is empty, and if I cannot sleep in that, you must provide me some other place, for I will not put up any longer with the vermin in my present abode."

"Sleep in the garden hut, by all means," he replied, "and you can have your food in the kitchen with the girls."

I was satisfied with this arrangement, and found myself in much more comfortable circumstances.

Only a week had elapsed, however, when my master told me that I would in future be placed on outside rations.

"I will not agree to that," I said immediately. "You must give me as much to eat as I require."

"I will give you as much as I allow the other men," he replied. "The allowance is 12lbs. flour, 12lbs. meat, 2lbs. sugar, and a ¼lb. tea."

"Meat, do you call it?" I exclaimed. "Why, you have so many sheep on your run that your mutton is thin enough to see through; and the mahogany that you have been supplying out of your store instead of fresh meat is as hard as a stone, and has been in salt for years. It is only to-day," I continued, "that one of your men was complaining about it, and seeing a pig outside the hut, he threw his share of meat at the animal, with the result that the pig dropped dead from the effects of the blow, and if you doubt my word, you may easily convince yourself of the truth."

"Tell me the name of that man," he demanded, "and so surely as I am a justice of the peace, I'll give him a severe sentence."

"I shall not tell you," I replied. "You have no right to issue such meat, and you deserve to lose the pig for your meanness. You will not gain an advantage over me, though, and if you don't allow me to continue to sleep in the garden hut and have my meals in the kitchen, you must put up with the consequences. Oppresion in gaol was the means of getting me a life sentence, and I am therefore not likely to stand oppression out of gaol."

This outspoken speech had the desired effect, and he assured me that he would not alter my present habits, and also that he would abide by a former promise he had made me, and give me the same money as ticket-of-leave men and free men during the harvest.

The harvesting season at length arrived, and lasted over thirty days. In that time I had averaged an acre daily, for which I was paid £1 per acre, so that I had a decent sum to draw. Out of this money I ordered a dress suit from a tailor in Spring Bay, two pairs of Wellington boots from another shopkeeper, and also requested my master, who was about to visit Hobart Town, to procure me a tweed suit and two portmanteaux.

I now thought it time to come to some definite arrangement as to the amount of wages I would receive as a passholder. On a Sunday morning, therefore, after my master had served out the week's rations to the men, I sought a private interview with him. I had an idea that he would press me to stay for small wages, and I prepared myself for emergencies. During my leisure time I had manufactured a piece of iron into the shape of a sword in the blacksmith's shop on the farm, to which I affixed a handle. This weapon I had concealed on me when I waited on my master.

"Well, Mark, he replied, "I'll give you £12 per year as you are a good man, and that is £3 more than you are entitled to."

"Twelve pounds per year!" I exclaimed indignantly, "after having done as much reaping as two men! Forty pounds is what I want, and if I were paid as I deserve you would give me £60. I am looking forward to a prosperous time, and I assure you I shall not allow you to take advantage of my position."

"But look at your future prospects!" he remarked persuasively. "In six months time I will get your ticket-of-leave, and you will then receive the same wages as a free man, viz., £40 per year. Then you are going to marry the servant girl Margaret," he continued, "and when that happy event transpires you can rent the farm my brother occupied from me, and make your fortune."

I told him that my future prospects had nothing to do with him. I wanted £40 a year, or I would not stay with him. Then my blood began to get hot at the thought of this man reaping the advantage of my superior strength and ability, and I told him my opinion of him, and demanded my discharge.

"Your tyrannical conduct is well known," I continued. "It was the prisoners from Maria Island whom you ground down in order to secure your property; but you wont add to your fortune by my exertions. I have been the brave hero of England!" I added, drawing my weapon from its concealment and brandishing it ominously over his head, "and I am the brave hero of Tasmania! Write me my discharge, or I will give you what I have given others."

I warned him not to alarm the special constable on the farm, but his wife, who had entered the room during our conversation, screamed out—

"James, James, for God's sake give him his discharge! I can see something desperate in the man's face."

Being thus prevailed upon, he sat down and cooly wrote my discharge to return to the barracks, which he then handed me. It was Sunday morning, however, and I said I would not leave until the following morning.

"But, beware," I added. "Don't send to Spring Bay for the police. If you get me a sentence, I will take to the bush when I come out, and wait for you behind a tree when you are going to Spring Bay to sit on the bench. The first ball will go through your horse, the next through your body, and I will then finish you off with a cutlass."

He assured me that he would not inform against me, as he was only too glad to be rid of such a dangerous man; a promise he faithfully fulfilled.

CHAPTER XVI.

Mr. Grueber—Frightening a Constable—Cheap Services— A Pair of Desperadoes—A Difficult Arrest—The Fruits of Good Conduct.

On the following morning I turned my back on Mr. ——'s farm and journeyed towards Hobart Town. Before reaching Prosser's Plains, however, I ascertained that Mr. Stephen Grueber was building a new barn, and hearing that he bore an excellent character amongst his men, I determined to wait on him.

I was neatly attired, wearing one of my new suits and a beaver hat. On knocking at the door and asking for Mr. Grueber I was informed by the mistress of the house that I would find him in an adjoining paddock.

On meeting the gentleman I was in search of he asked me who I was and the nature of my business, whereupon I replied—

"A full-blown passholder in search of work."

I told him I had been informed that he was having a new barn built and so thought he might find me something to do. I also disclosed to him all that had occurred between Mr. —— and myself.

He appeared pleased with me and promised that if I could obtain work for a few weeks at Mr. Dan Simpson's, who lived close by, he would afterwards employ me; at the same time he stated that he would not take advantage of my position, nor see me idle if Mr. Simpson had nothing for me to do.

As it happened that gentleman did not require my services, and I continued on in the direction of Prosser's Plains before deciding to return to Mr. Grueber. As I was crossing the creek I saw a constable filling a kettle with water.

"Who are you?" he shouted out as I approached him.

I rushed across the creek and made a pretence to strike him, upon which he appeared terribly frightened.

'I don't mean any offence, I assure you," he said.

This remark quelled any fear of danger that had existed in my mind. Then I asked him as to employment, and he informed me that a Mr. Ashton, the district constable, wanted a man to cook for him.

I immediately went in the direction of that person's house, and related my story to Mr. Ashton, informing him, of course, that my services would be required by Mr. Grueber in a few weeks.

"I wanted an old man," he remarked.

I laughed at this admission, for I could perceive by his manner that he wished to obtain the services of a man for a few shillings a week. But I was in a good humour at the time, and startled him by exclaiming—

"I'll work for you for nothing until Mr. Grueber requires me."

He readily accepted this proposition, and I was at once installed in my new duties.

After a few days satisfactory service under him a man named Burridge, who got his living by kangarooing in the neighbourhood, caused us a great deal of trouble. He had as a companion a man who was called "Frenchy,'- and they bore a very ill name. Some time previous to the incident I am about to relate, they had been apprehended on a charge of killing a constable and staking him to the ground. The policeman was on his way to Mr. Grueber's house with despatches, when he espied the men killing a settler's sheep, and in trying to effect their arrest, he met with the treatment above described. I remember Dr. Coverdale speaking about the murder, and he told me that though the evidence was not sufficiently strong to convict them, it was generally believed that they were the guilty parties.

The trouble on this occasion arose out of a visit we had from Burridge's wife, who told the district constable that her husband and "Frenchy," who had been drinking heavily, had attempted to take her life, at the same time pointing to her wrist, which had been severely injured with a knife. She feared them greatly, and desired the constable to arrest them.

Mr. Ashton turned to me and said—"I know you will assist me to arrest this pair."

"No," I replied; "I will not risk my life for what you are paid to do. Moreover, you are not justified in arresting them on the complaint of the woman."

After a little persuasion, I agreed to accompany him, and Mr. Moore, the watch-house keeper, also joined us.

We proceeded to the house, and on knocking at the hall door, Burridge, who was in a sitting-room on the right-hand side, called out—

"Who's there?"

"It is I, Mr. Ashton," replied the constable.

On hearing the reply, Burridge invited him inside, and the constable entered the door, followed by Mr. Moore, I remaining outside.

A moment afterwards I heard the sounds of a scuffle, and the exclamation, "Mark! Mark!" I ran inside to render assistance, and perceived that a desperate fight was taking place.

Burridge had a double-barrelled gun in his possession, and he was making strenuous efforts to use this weapon. No sooner had I taken in the scene than I rushed towards Burridge, and quickly wrested the gun from his grasp.

At that instant "Frenchy" also suddenly took his weapon down from the wall.

"Shove that gun across the floor to me and sit down," I thundered forth, pointing the gun I had in my hand at him, "or I'll give you the contents of both barrels."

He was wise enough to obey my orders and I then took guard over him.

During this time the constable and Mr. Moore were engaged on Burridge, and the heat of the encounter had by no means diminished. He kicked and bit them, and tried in every way to escape. Up and down they went, and the struggle was almost laughable, for they were puffing and snorting like a team of jaded horses.

At last Mr. Ashton retired from the contest and came over to me.

"Give me the piece," he said, "and let me look after 'Frenchy' while you give Moore a hand."

I told him he would have been in a pretty fix if I had not consented to accompany him. Then, turning to Burridge, I told him that his wife had laid a charge against him, and the best thing he could do was to go quietly.

"I am bound to 'aid and assist,' according to law," I added, "though I don't like the job."

Burridge replied to this advice by whipping his arms around me and trying to bite me. I immediately gave him a severe blow behind the ear, which had the effect of dazing him He continued to fight, however, until I knocked him down twice, and recommended him not to resist again.

We eventually got the pair locked up, and Burridge was charged with brutality to his wife, there being also a separate charge against the two men of resisting the police while in the execution of their duty.

Three justices of the peace were appealed to, and the case being heard, the men were committed for trial at the Hobart Town Criminal Sessions. I subsequently heard, however, that the Attorney-General did not file a bill against them.

When I desired to leave Mr. Ashton's service, there was quite a scene, and he and his wife did their utmost to prevail upon me to remain with them. Their child had grown fond of me, and I was always partial to children. I, however, refused to remain, even though Mr. Ashton promised to get me a situation as a constable at 5/10 per day, adding that he would remove the assistant he had at that time so that I would be able to reside with him.

I had not completed enough of my sentence to entitle me to a conditional pardon; but Mr. Ashton, in a long letter to the Executive, submitted a full account of my behaviour, and strongly recommended the consideration of my case for meritorious conduct.

To this a reply was received that my ticket would be granted in five years and eight months, and further notified that I was to apply for a conditional pardon twelve months after the expiration of that term.

After I left Mr. Ashton I returned to Mr. Grueber and was engaged at threshing at sixpence per bushel. I managed to earn about eight or nine shillings a day at that employment, and was also well treated and fed.

CHAPTER XVII.

A New Master—A Love Episode and Its Effects—Rough Merriment—"I Want My Discharge"—Too Rowdy— The Results of a Drinking Bout—A Sentence Back to Port Arthur.

After leaving Mr. Grueber's employ, in 1855, I went to the watch-house keeper at Richmond and gave in my residence, telling him that I was going to thresh for Mr. Murdoch, whose farm was situated between Richmond and Kangaroo Point.

When I waited on that gentleman, however, he informed me that he was building a new barn, which would be completed in a week, and requested me to call after the lapse of that interval.

Returning to Richmond, I obtained accommodation at a hotel. On the appointed day, I prepared to revisit Mr. Murdoch, and, suffering from an artificial elevation of spirits, I dressed in my best suit, beaver hat, and a light fashionable overcoat, a bottle of rum peeping from each of the pockets of the latter.

On reaching the house, I introduced myself to Mrs. Murdoch and the nursemaid as "Newmarket John, one of the nonesuch." I told her that I was a fortune teller, having travelled with Anderson, "Wizard of the North," when in England. After my charts arrived, I added, I was going to make some money, marry a native girl, and take her home to the old country with me.

The servant girl, who was only about sixteen years of age, listened to my foolish remarks with much interest, and they subsequently proved a source of much trouble to me.

Mrs. Murdoch said it was a pity to see a man of my appearance in drink, and advised me to save my money and buy a farm.

On interviewing Mr. Murdoch, he informed me that the temporary barn was finished, and that he had also engaged two men to thresh in another barn. Having purchased a farm in Queensland, however, he wanted the work done as speedily as possible, to enable him to leave the country, hence he engaged me at eightpence a bushel. Wheat was at this time fetching £1 per bushel, so that he was in a position to pay well for the threshing.

As Newmarket John, I started work early on the Monday morning, and had not been long engaged at it when Mr. Murdoch, and a gentleman named Mr. Hardinge, who was going to rent the farm after the former's departure, said I was doing my work uncommonly well, at the same time pronouncing me a powerful man. By the end of the week I had threshed eighty bushels, thereby earning £2 13/4.

Every day the young girl who was employed at the house as nursemaid came to see me, with the child in her arms, and on each occasion her earnest request was that I should marry her. She told me that she was born in Macquarie street, Hobart Town, where her stepmother then lived, and that her own father had left her a few hundred pounds, of which she would become possessed when she came of age.

I did my best to disabuse her mind of my desire to marry a native girl, but I could not rid myself of her company until the mistress came and called her away.

On several occasions Mrs. Murdoch spoke to me about the girl's conduct.

"Well, what can I do with the girl?" was my reply. "You should correct her, for I can't keep her away."

On leaving my work one evening to go to the homestead for tea the girl came to me while I was having a preliminary wash, and complained bitterly that her mistress had been hitting her, but vowing, if she was struck again that she would retaliate.

"If you don't run away with me," she added; "I will run away myself and get married."

I advised her to go away before she got me into disgrace, but without avail, and as I sat on the bench where I had been washing, she flung both her arms round my neck.

Her mistress came out at this moment, and, perceiving the girl so affectionately embracing me, said—

"Now, Newmarket John, I am surprised at you permitting that girl to hug you in the way she is doing."

"The girl is too rowdy," I replied, "like many more of the Tasmanian natives. She is not kept in her proper place, so what am I to do with her?"

Hot words ensued, and ultimately I expressed my intention to rid myself of the girl by leaving my employment in the morning.

When I saw Mr. Murdoch I requested him to pay me for the work I had done, two or three days being owing to me at the time.

"Never mind the girl," he urged. "I will arrange matters as to prevent her bothering you in future. I will not let her out when the men are about, and as you are a good workman, you had better stop where you are."

I emphatically assured him that I would not remain in his service any longer, as the mistress had insulted me, and I did not intend to be insulted by anyone.

When Mr. Murdoch found that he could not prevail upon me to stay, he asked me how much I expected for the work I had done. I mentioned the sum, whereupon he replied that it was too much, and that I would first have to dress the work up with a machine and measure it.

"I will not stay in your employ another minute," I replied, "and if you do not let me go it will be a bad job for you."

I also informed him of my real name, and when he perceived that I was getting into a rage he paid me what I asked, and I immediately left the homestead.

A tenant of Mr. Murdoch's, who lived on the same estate, had at the time between three and four hundred bushels of wheat to thresh, and I proceeded to his place and arranged to do the work. The name of this person was Dennis King, and he had only recently been married. He was a wild harum-scarum young fellow, and I had no sooner agreed to work for him, than he invited me to accompany him into Richmond, adding that I could start work on the morrow.

Having reached the township, I proceeded to the watch-house keeper and informed him that I had left Mr. Murdoch's employ, and had agreed to enter that of Dennis King.

He stated that he would not receive my change of residence until I presented my discharge from my late employer.

Mr. Murdoch, I may state, was not aware that I was a passholder; neither had I told King my real name, as I desired to conceal my position.

Having left the watch-house keeper, I accompanied King to several public-houses. We entered the respective parlours, and thoroughly enjoyed ourselves for a time. On starting homewards King was intoxicated, whilst I was in a state of merriment and full of life.

When we had got about a mile out of Richmond, I commenced to sing a song, and meeting a gentleman—whom I subsequently found to be a police magistrate—on the road, accompanied by two ladies, I accosted him, and requested his opinion of my song.

He called me a blackguard, and with that I gave him a playful spank on the face, asking him jocularly how he dared insult me.

The gentleman called lustily for the police, and I took to my heels and ran towards Mr. Murdoch's. King followed to the best of his ability, but as I rapidly outstripped him, I waited for him on the roadside.

On nearing Mr. Murdoch's house I parted from King, promising to rejoin him in half-an-hour. On reaching my destination, I opened the door, walked in, and called out for Mr. Murdoch. The men by this time had retired for the night.

"What do you want, John?" Mr. Murdoch demanded.

"My discharge," I replied.

"You do not require any discharge," said he.

"I certainly do," I persisted. "Have I to remind you again that my name is Mark Jeffrey, and not Newmarket John?"

On hearing this, he went inside, and writing my discharge brought it out to me.

Being still elevated from the effects of the liquor I had imbibed, I commenced to poke fun at the document, pointing out where he had spelt my name wrong.

He then snatched the paper out of my hand, but he had no sooner done so than I sent him sprawling on the floor with my fist.

Mr. Hardinge, who was present, picked up a billet of firewood, which was lying in the kitchen, and with it struck me a severe blow unawares on the forehead, splitting it open and leaving me senseless. I was carried into the barn, where I stayed for the night.

When I awoke in the morning my face was swollen, my eyes had turned black, and I was spitting blood from the effects of the blow. It was about eight o'clock when I jumped up and recollected the scene of the previous night. I made for the kitchen, but the inmates no sooner perceived my approach than they barricaded the door.

Running to the wood heap, I cut a piece of wood before making an attempt to enter the kitchen. I gave the door three or four kicks, but failed to force it open. Next, I tried the window; but just as I had got one blow at it, Mr. Murdoch fired the contents of a fowling-piece at me, and instructed his brother to go to Kangaroo Point and fetch a constable, it being his intention to give me in charge.

Deeming discretion the better part of valour, I took to my heels and ran towards Richmond, which place I reached long before young Murdoch could obtain the constable.

I proceeded to Mr. Wilmott, the police magistrate who was on the bench that morning, and made application to summons my late master for refusing to give me my discharge, and Hardinge for assaulting me.

Just as the summonses had been drawn out, the constable came running in, stating that my late master had instructed him to apprehend me.

Mr. Wilmott, however, handed him the two summonses for delivery, they being made returnable in a few days.

He notified me to appear on that day, and stated that in the meantime he would take no further action.

Felicitating myself on the narrow escape I had undergone, I made my way to Murphy's public-house, and, entering the parlour, called for a bottle of ale and some bread and cheese.

While relishing this refreshment, the magistrate whom I had accosted on the previous evening entered the room, accompanied by two constables.

"That's the man who asaulted me and frightened the two ladies!" he said, addressing the constables and pointing at the same time to me. "Take him to the watch-house."

Ere they had time to fulfil this command, however, I had jumped to my feet and sent both policemen head over-heels, upon which the magistrate beat an undignified retreat.

The publican then came to the rescue, and having discomforted him by a severe blow, I was effecting my escape, when a number of men who were in the bar at the time rushed towards me and prevented me from gaining my liberty.

By this time the constables had recovered their self-possession, and, following me into the tap-room, achieved my arrest.

The following morning I was charged with the assault, and received a sentence of nine months. Therefore, when Mr. Murdoch and Mr. Hardinge appeared in answer to their summonses, I was in prison, but was brought up in custody to give evidence against them.

At the conclusion of the evidence, Mr. Wilmott, who presided, remarked that he wished he had been in possession of the facts of the case before he had issued the summonses.

I was then taken out of court while the bench formed their decision, and after a lapse of a quarter of an hour was placed in the dock once more, and my previous sentence increased from nine to eighteen months.

To undergo this term of confinement, I was transferred to Port Arthur.

CHAPTER XVIII.

Old Tyranny Revived—A Determined Protest—An Additional Sentence—Sir Henry Fox Young—A Sentence Cancelled—Life at the Peninsula—A Mean Proposal.

Port Arthur once more!

No wonder that on this occasion I felt some degree of compunction for the folly that had again guided me into this vile abode of wretchedness and woe. Opportunities had offered themselves to redeem the ignominious name I bore—to elevate my standpoint in the battle of life—but these advantages I had thoughtlessly spurned, and I was thrust deeper than ever into the dangerous complications surrounding on every side a protracted term of enforced imprisonment in the companionship of other hardened criminals.

I was placed in one of the hardest-worked gangs of the settlement—that known as the wood gang—where the prisoners were employed to fell trees, cut them into two-feet lengths, split them into billets, and stack the wood in divisions of fourteen feet long and five feet in height.

In this work I had frequent disagreements with my fellow-prisoners, as none of them had the ability to keep pace with me.

Sullen murmurings were heard on every hand, for it was an unpleasant task for those of the men who exerted their utmost efforts throughout the day only to find that they had failed in their allotted duty, and to consequently have to undergo a sentence of solitary confinement.

The commandant (Mr. James Boyd) exercised supreme power, and no plea or excuse would have the effect of diverting the penalty attached to a failure in completing the regulation quantity of work.

When I had served four of the eighteen months I had been sentenced to, the commandant issued instructions that two prisoners were to be appointed as delegates each day after dinner, whose duty was to remain in the cook-house, and see that none of the rations were illegitimately disposed of, but that every prisoner should receive his proper allowance of food.

This regulaiton had been brought into force chiefly on account of a system which obtained amongst the cooks of fraudulently depriving the prisoners of a portion of their allowance, and disposing of it to persons residing outside the settlement. The practice had been exposed through some of the men having been detected gambling for money, and in the consequent trials which ensued, suspicions were aroused as to the means whereby they obtained these funds.

The system of appointing delegates, however, proved in my estimation a very unfair one. The same men were selected for the duty day after day, whilst I considered that the duties should devolve more equally upon the "fleet," especially as the evil showed no abatement.

Fully impressed with this conviction, I, one day, in the company of a prisoner named Haley, suggested to the muster master that my companion and myself should be allowed to fill the post of delegates, at the same time expressing my determination to remedy the abuse.

"No one but favourites are elected to the position," I remarked, "and it is high time that more decisive measures were taken."

"If you do not return to your gang," said the muster-master, "I will have you locked up."

I had fully expected this intimation, but I was not to be baffled so easily.   Haley, however, on hearing the threat, at once lost heart, and hastily resumed his former position.

"You can lock me up or do what you choose," was my reply, "but I demand to be appointed a delegate"

My persistency had the desired effect, for he foresaw that the justness of my request would considerably injure him if he were to bring a charge of insubordination against me.

"Have it your own way," he replied with a shrug of his shoulders, and he then appointed another prisoner to accompany me.

When I reported myself to Mr. Smith, the overseer of the bakery and cookhouse, he referred me to a copy of the rules, which stated that the delegates were to assist the cooks in their duties.

"Well," I replied, "I shall pay no heed to such a rule. The delegates are appointed to see that every prisoner has his proper allowance of food, and it is impossible for them to detect dishonesty among the cooks unless they are allowed their own latitude."

"But it is the commandant's orders that you are to work," he rejoined.

"If that is the case," I said, "the commandant has formulated that rule blindly, for it gives you and your subordinates an opportunity of defrauding the men.   But rather than abide by it, I will suffer the consequences."

On hearing this point-blank assertion, he sent for two constables and gave me in cha regfor refusing to work.

The following morning I was brought before the commandant, who would hear nothing in extenuation of the charge.   He imposed upon me an additional sentence of six months, which I was to undergo in the Model Prison. This term was to be preceded by fourteen days solitary confinement, and he further stated that he would recommend the Executive Council to retain me in the Model Prison until further orders.

The severity of this punishment will be understood by those who are conversant with the rigid discipline which existed in this institution.   The prisoners were placed in separate cells, and intercourse between each other was strictly prohibited.   Even when exercising in the yard the men were compelled to wear masks with eyelet-holes, so that the only faces a prisoner saw were those of the constables and warders.

Whilst I was undergoing confinement in the Model Prison, Sir Henry Fox Young (the then Governor) made a visit to the institution for the purpose of personally hearing any complaints prisoners had to make.

His Excellency was a fair and dispassionate gentleman, and when I was brought before him he listened patiently to the grievances I had to unfold.

I explained to him the systematic manner in which the prisoners were robbed of their food, adding that if he would peruse the charge books he would find my statements substantiated by the number of cases 'brought against the offenders.

The Governor immediately sent for the books, and on examining them said that he found my statements fully borne out.

I then pointed out to him the impossibility of the cooks fraudulently disposing of the meat had the commandant not included the proviso I objected to, but simply left the delegates to perform their proper duty.

"For this protest," I added, "I have been sentenced to six months confinement in this prison."

"Surely, commandant," said his Excellency, turning to that individual, "you do not expect the delegates to perform a double duty? How can they be responsible for the food if they are compelled to work?"

The prison official was considerably perturbed at these questions, and I seized the momentary advantage to point an accusing finger at him and say—

"Observe his embarrassment, your Excellency. The rule is only a subterfuge. He finds too much pleasure in having prisoners brought before him to frame any measures for lessening crime."

Two other unjust sentences I had undergone whilst in the wood gang I brought under the notice of the Governor, who gave an attentive ear to my complaints.

"Well, my man," he said at length, "I will see into your case."

This reply was not altogether satisfactory.

"I humbly trust that your Excellency will see into it at once," I urged. "I am in the lions mouth, and the commandant will take further advantage of me for having made these complaints. All I ask for is protection in accordance with the law of the land, and to have the unjust sentence imposed upon me remitted."

His Excellency stated that I could rely upon his assurance that my case would be seen into, and that justice would be meted out to me.

This proved no empty promise, for on the following day, to my intense satisfaction and the evident discomfiture of the commandant, I was ordered to be released from the Model Prison and my additional sentence was also cancelled.

I was then sent out to the mines at the Peninsula, in the situation of woodcutter and attendant on three constables. My new post was some distance from the settlement, and in order to reach it I had to pass through the Cascades, Impresion Bay, and Saltwater River.

On my road I became acquainted with one or two persons, from whom I learnt that the senior constable to whom I was billeted was strict and tyrannical, and that I would have to be on my guard.

When I reported myself, however, I found his nature to be quite the reverse of that described. He was extremely affable, and told me that my duties simply consisted in keeping the fires alight, and taking in water. For this purpose there was no necessity to chop wood, as there was any amount of slack coal near the house. He also told me that as long as I carried out the stated duty he would be satisfied, and that I could please myself whether or not I cooked for the constables.

The name of the senior constable was Hancock, and, as he had no nose, his appearance was greatly against him. Having completed a sentence, he had been appointed petty constable, subsequently rising to the post he held at the time of my arrival.

After a short period, I contracted a warm friendship with one of the constables whose name was Herod. He was accustomed to set kangaroo snares at Black Jack, a few miles from Saltwater River, and on one occasion, at his request, I accompanied him, in order to assist him in carrying home the game he expected to find entrapped.

We found three kangaroos and six wallabies, and on taking them home and skinning them, Herod liberally offered to give me an equal division of the profits of that and similar speculations in the future, a proposal I willingly accepted.

Herod then suggested that I should cook for him, as on the day previous to this incident I had invited him to a dinner of my own preparation, which he had greatly enjoyed. I acceded to his request and stated that as the other petty constable (Bates) was also a good-hearted fellow I was willing to cook for him also. This amicable agreement was entered into and matters progressed in good fellowship for some time afterwards.

One day, however, the senior constable observed me coming out of a miner's house, where I had been transacting the sale of a kangaroo. Hancock, who used to stutter very much, said, "If I catch you in this miner's house again I shall have to take you before the commandant."

I laughed at him, and told him that as I was on legitimate business, he could take me before the commandant when he thought fit to do so; but that I would afterwards repay him for his trouble in a manner he little thought of.

My avowal was the means of conciliating him, and he remarked that there was no occasion for me to be offended, as he had only spoken in jest.

I then told him the nature of my business with the miner, and asked him if he had any objection to the constable and myself snaring and selling kangaroo.

He assured me that he had not, and gave me full permission to continue the occupation.

Whether the senior constable had the courage of his own opinions I know not, but it appeared to me somewhat peculiar that during the same week Herod should receive orders for removal to another station.

On taking his departure he presented me with the kangaroo snares, the skins we had on hand, and a half-sovereign, and I felt exceedingly sorry to part with such an open-hearted and sociable young fellow.

A man named McGuire, who had only recently been discharged from prison, was appointed to fill the vacancy. I took a natural dislike to him, and, finding him to be extremely selfish and fretful, I left him to manage his own cooking.

About this time Mr. Thompson, who was connected with the mines, turned insolvent, and, for some reason not affecting me, the senior constable kept back a cow and a butter churn from the sale.

This came to the knowledge of McGuire, and he requested me to associate with him in reporting Hancock, adding that he would amply compensate me. Being well-educated, he was in hopes that this fact, taken into consideration with the report he was about to make, would be the means of causing him to be appointed as Hancock's successor.

To this request I gave a most emphatic refusal, stating that not only did I object to such a vile conspiracy, but, that as the senior constable had never interfered with me, I was not going to meddle in matters concerning his public or private business.

So indignant, in fact, did I feel at this unmanly proposal, that I sought an immediate interview with Hancock, and acquainted him with McGuire's conduct.

The senior constable appeared in no way disconcerted at the knowledge we possessed concerning the butter churn and cow. On the other hand he seemed to court investigation, for he at once sat down and wrote a despatch to the settlement.

"I will soon remove him, Mark," he said, and he was true to his word, for on the following day he had the satisfaction of giving McGuire his marching orders, and Martin Cash, the erstwhile bushranger, was appointed in his stead.

CHAPTER XIX.

A Successful Baker—More Conspiracy—The Romance of a Dress Suit—Attempted Murder—The "Bush Law-yah" Acts Cunning—A Brave Warder—Amusing the Bench—Repaid with Solitary Confinement.

After the insolvency referred to in the previous chapter, Mr. Husk resumed control of the mines, and as he had omitted to engage a man to bake for the miners he brought with him, I had an opportunity of displaying a practical knowledge of the art of bakery.

I waited on Mr. Husk and informed him of my competency to manufacture bread, and also to make my own yeast ,expressing my willingness to bake a batch for him whenever he required, provided he sent a man to assist me, the remuneration I expected on each occasion being half-a-sovereign and a bottle of rum.

He not only agreed to my terms, but also promised that I should have the additional assistance of his wife.

There was a large oven connected with the place, which was capable of taking between three hundred and four hundred loaves. At my first attempt I turned out about two hundred and fifty loaves, and the result of my efforts was highly appreciated by the men, who stated that they had never tasted such good bread even in Hobart Town.

So successful was I, in fact, that Mr. Husk offered to engage me permanently as soon as the short remainder of my sentence had expired at 50s. per week, but as such a situation was not to my taste, I assured him that I would not remain if he gave me £5 per week.

Hancock, the senior constable, one day received information that some prisoners in the bush were building a boat with the object of escaping from the mainland, and, taking one of the constables with him, he went away to investigate the matter.

A few hours after his departure a passholder named Morton, but who was more generally known as the "Waterloo Fifer"—having been engaged in the Battle of Waterloo——appeared on the scene.

He stated that he had "signalised" for me to be taken into the settlement to give evidence as to Hancock selling a Mrs. Newcombe some blankets.

I informed him that he was under a misapprehension, as the articles had not been sold Hancock had simply lent them to the lady until the arrival of the next conveyance, and they had been duly returned by her servant.

"Well," said Morton, "if you confirm my statement to the commandant that they were sold, then I shall be made senior constable, and will give you a five-pound note for your trouble."

"I will have nothing to do with it," I replied. "Moreover, I would be certain to incriminate myself, as the blankets have been returned, and the commandant is sure to send a 'confidential man' out here to see if the number

of blankets is correct As you have signalised for me to
be taken in," I continued, "of course I will have to go, but
I shall certainly tell the commandant the truth, and also
that there has been an altercation between you and Hancock relative to duty."

Knowing from experience that it was more than probable that I would commit myself in some way in giving
evidence before the commandant, I took with me, on the
journey to the settlement with Morton, a black cloth suit,
which I had procured in anticipation of regaining my
liberty once more. On reaching Saltwater River, I entrusted the clothes to an acquaintance named Bob Anderson, instructing him to send them on to a friend of mine
in the settlement if I were placed under restraint.

When before the commandant, I gave my evidence in
strict conformity with the truth, and, as I had surmised,
he immediately sent out a "confidential man" ahead of us
to see if the number of blankets was correct, and we met
him on our return journey, when he certified that they
were all accounted for.

As soon as we arrived at Saltwater River, I reclaimed
the suit I had entrusted to Bob Anderson; but judge of
my surprise when, upon reaching our destination, Morton
vindictively gave me in charge for having the clothes in
my possesion without being able to give a satisfactory
account of how I obtained them.

"I must take the charge, Mark," said Hancock, before
whom I was taken, "and lock you up till to-morrow morning."

Of course I was aware that duty compelled him to take
this step, and so I submitted to this new indignity without
resistance.

The following morning I was escorted to the settlement
by Morton and placed on trial before the commandant.

Morton swore that on returning to the mines I took the
suit from a prisoner-baker named Anderson, at Saltwater
River, and when he had concluded his statement I was
asked if I had anything to stay in my defence, or any
questions to ask.

"You said I got the suit at the river?" I enquired of
Morton.

"Yes, I did," he replied.

I then asked him why, being a constable, he did not
arrest me at that time, when I would have had an opportunity of proving my innocence.

He was evidently too much confused to reply to this
question, when the commandant, perceiving his hesitation,
interposed on his behalf.

"Ah! Dangerous man, Morton! Frightened of him, eh?"
he said, with the peculiar drawl and intonation habitual
to him.

"Yes, commandant," replied Morton, in tones like a
whining schoolboy.

"If I am as dangerous as represented," I remarked,
turning to the commandant, "there are three other constables stationed at Saltwater River, and if Morton was

afraid to effect my arrest he could have secured their services. You see, sir, he is conspiring against me because I did not corroborate the evidence he gave against Hancock."

"Silence, sah!" exclaimed the commandant. "Too much of a bush lawyah!"

He added that I was always extricating myself from charges of which he believed me to be guilty. He was heartily tired of listening to the rebutting points I submitted, and he sincerely trusted that he would not have to undergo another ordeal of a similar nature. The best thing he could do with me, he thought, was to send me to the railway huts, where I would have to run the wagons.

"I beg to remind you," I remarked, 'that Dr. Seccombe and Dr. Brownwell have both exempted me from running, in consequence of my having dislocated my ankle between the wheel spokes and body of a cart when a boy, and that my leg is therefore incapable of violent exertion."

"If you give me any more insolence, sah," he exclaimed. "I will send you to the Model Prison! Take him away, constable."

I was accordingly removed from the august presence of the commandant, and at about noon was placed under the armed escort at Morton, without handcuffs, to be conducted to my new sphere of labour. But I was determined not to proceed hither without putting forth an effort to wreak vengeance on Morton, and an opportunity son presented itself.

When we reached a place called Brickfield Hill, situated about half a mile from the settlement, a heavy shower of rain began to fall. The brickmakers had gone to dinner, and we therefore took shelter under one of the sheds beneath which the bricks were laid in a hollow to dry.

Morton took up a positin with his back to the stack of bricks, from whence he could obtain a view of the roadside; but as I was confronting him, my back was necessarily turned to the road, and I was therefore unable to see passers by; still there was nobody in view when we turned from it.

My escort suggested that we should have a smoke. I consented, and he was in the act of proffering me a clay pipe, when I seized the barrel of his piece with my left hand, and the stock with my right hand.

He strove to retain his hold of the weapon, but by a dexterous movement I spun him in the air, and he descended on the stack of soft bricks.

Ere I could prevent his utterance, he had shrieked out "Murder!" with all the lustiness of a man placed in his position; but he had no opportunity to repeat the cry, for I pinned him by the throat and held him there until he was almost breathless.

I had relaxed my grasp and was about to rise from my recumbent position, having obtained possession of the gun, when I received a heavy blow from behind on the back of the ear.

It sent me sprawling to mother earth, and in my fall the weapon slipped from my hands. I quickly regained my feet, however, and then found that I had been interrupted in carrying out my revenge by a soldier, who, in passing along the road, had been attracted by Morton's call for aid.

When I perceived the threatening attitude of my new assailant, and also observed that my victim was rapidly recovering, I took to my heels at a swing pace, notwithstanding the dislocated ankle.

This movement had been anticipated, however, and the soldier immediately presented his piece.

"Halt! or I fire!" he shouted.

"Fire and be hanged!" I thundered back with a yell of defiance.

Indistinctly I could hear the click of the hammer, but instead of the impending report, it was followed by a volley of oaths from the soldier.

The weapon, I afterwards ascertained, had become caked with soft clay, and it was therefore temporarily useless.

At the top of my speed I hastened to the watch-house, and laid a charge against Morton for assaulting me, and the soldier for having struck me viciously with a stick.

Owing to the force with which I had thrown Morton, my wrist was severely swollen, and this I exhibited as proof of the assault.

But whilst I was laying the charge, both of my late opponents entered the guard-room, and submitted their version of the incident. The senior constable at once directed that I should be conveyed to the Model Prison on the charge of attempted murder.

On the ensuing day I was brought before Dr. Seccombe and Dr. Brownwell, when the soldier, in a much longer story than was necessary, preferred against me the charge of wilful intent, stating that I would most assuredly have killed Morton had he not interfered so opportunely.

In cross-examination I asked the constable what position I was in when he came up and struck me with the stick.

"You were just rising off the man," he replied, "having the piece in your hands."

"How, then, can you swear that I was about to kill the man?" I returned. "You are unable to say whether or not he assaulted me, but had you been a minute later you would have seen me leading him handcuffed to the watch-house on a charge of that nature."

The bench at this stage indulged in a hearty laugh, but whether the statement bore a ludicrous aspect, or whether they doubted my veracity, I cannot say.

"We do not know what to make of you!" one of the jurors remarked. "You are always in trouble, and you invariably come into Court with the air of an injured man. Did you not get fourteen days in Safety Cove for molesting a warder in charge of the station there?"

"Yes, your Worship," I answered, with a burst of indignation; "but it was a very unjust sentence. The warder had a pistol and he was showing it to some of his friends. I was standing near him at the time, and I think he was desirous that I should overhear his conversation. He said, your Worships, that I was always grumbling about my rations and threatening him, but that if I attempted to injure him he would shoot me like a dog. I simply made a pretence of rushing towards him in order to test his bravery, but he immediately dropped the pistol and ran away, calling for assistance. The constables came up and, although I was enjoying the joke at the time, your Worships, they arrested me and I got fourteen days."

Another titter of incredulity hovered for a moment around the judicial bench, and they then said they hardly knew how to treat the case.

"Discharge me and put the soldier on his trial for assault," I suggested, with outraged dignity.

The Bench, however, did not feel disposed to adopt this arbitrary course, but after a little whispering between themselves, sentenced me to thirty days solitary, on water and one pound of bread per diem.

CHAPTER XX.

A Good Samaritan—Sleek and "Belly Proud"—An Unjust Sentence—I Plot Murder Beyond the Prison Walls —Agricultural Pursuits—Too Frolicsome—A French Cook—Fritters v. Baked Meat and Potatoes—On Tramp Once More.

My term of thirty days solitary confinement was passed through under the most favourable auspices. One of the officials connected with the prison had become so impressed with my conduct relative to the Morton-Hancock episode that he took an opportunity of expressing his admiration, which he substantially evinced by secretly providing me with ample food during my confinement.

The visiting doctor also ordered me a mattress, owing to the pain I suffered from having exerted my ankle when beating a hasty retreat from the soldier and the constable. Therefore indolence and plenty for thirty days caused me to put on several pounds of flesh, and the authorities were considerably astonished when I finally issued from my cell in a sleek and "belly proud" condition.

But the pleasure of having escaped from a serious crime with such slight punishment was somewhat marred by the commandant informed me that the comptroller (Mr. Nairn) had, for my assault of Morton, decided to add another six months probation on the sentence I had to undergo before I could apply for my ticket-of-leave.

I vehemently protested against this outrage on British justice, pointing out how unfair it was that a man should be sentenced to additional punishment after having received satisfactory chastisement before the tribunal.

My argument appeared to have some effect on the commandant, for he promised that, as the comptroller would be visiting the settlement in a short time, I should have an interview with Mr. Nairn, to endeavour to prevail on him to rescind his decision.

In the meantime I was once more pressed into the wood gang, where I had ample time to chew the bitter cud of reflection.

The more my mind dwelt on this fresh indignity, the more I resolved to rebel against its fulfilment. I was goaded on to desperation, feeling once more that life was not worth living when my fellow-men took such inhuman advantage of my forlorn and degraded position by heaping persecution after persecution upon my head.

Filled with this strong impression, I firmly resolved that if the comptroller refused to annul the sentence I would murder him in cold blood—a prisoner could effect his object by no other means—and so for ever put an end to my miserable existence.

To prepare for this emergency, I obtained permission for a man to manufacture an iron instrument in the blacksmiths shop, under the plea that I was going to make grass brooms in my spare time. It was long and three-cornered like a bayonet, and about an inch and a half broad at the back. No suspicion was aroused by the manufacture of this instrument, for I had frequently made brooms for the institution, and I told the blacksmith that the tool would assist me to carry out the work more expeditiously.

When the comptroller arrived I was taken before him in the commandants private office. I explained to him the circumstances of Mortons conduct from the outset, and how he had conspired against me because of my refusal to assist him in ousting Hancock from his position as senior constable.

The comptroller listened to my remarks with interest, and fortunately, maybe, for him, extended clemency towards me. He stated that as the commandant had given me a good character since the time I had been sentenced to the term of thirty days solitary, he would remit the sentence, and have me conveyed to Hobart Town as soon as possible on ticket-of-leave.

I had concealed the weapon under my arm, between my shirt and vest, and I felt much relieved on finding that there was no necessity to use it. Had my case not received such favourable consideration, however, I would undoubtedly made a strenuous attempt to plunge it into the heart of the comptroller.

On being discharged from prison, and obtaining my ticket-of-leave, I worked at various places for about two years, nothing of moment transpiring during that time.

In the summer of 1859, I started from Hobart Town with the intention of proceeding to Launceston. On passing through New Town, however, I was accosted by the watch-house keeper, who, on learning that I was in search of employment, informed me that Mr. Walker, of Derwent Park, was in need of an able-bodied man who understood agricultural pursuits.

On interviewing the gentleman referred to, he stated that he did not require a man for a week or two, whereupon I pointed to several defects in his stacks, which had been caused by heavy thunderstorms, and warned him that if they were not remedied he would lose a lot of his hay.

This voluntary advice had a beneficial effect, for he engaged me to give immediate attention to the stacks, paying me at the rate of thirty shillings per week, with the best of living and as much half-and-half as I cared to drink.

I set to work and rectified the defects to his evident satisfaction, for on completing the task he presented me with a bonus of £5.

He then requested me to accept the overseership of his farm, at a salary of £150 annually and a comfortable place in which to reside.

This generous offer I refused, and bluntly informed him that I did not warrant such kindness and implicit confidence. I informed him of the bad habits I was addicted to, and pointed out that if I accepted an overseership I rendered myself liable to imprisonment for neglect of duty.

He thanked me for this outspoken candour, and then requested me to break up about four or five acres of virgin soil for him.

I inspected the ground, and finding it hard and stony, eventually agreed to undertake the work at the rate of £16 per acre.

During the period I was employed on this contract I rented a room from Mr. Cooley, of the Racehorse Hotel, New Town, which was situated about two miles from the farm. I averaged about £3 per week, breaking the ground to a depth of twelve inches.

The market price of mutton at this time was 2d. per lb., and for potatoes 2/- per cwt. My bread and groceries I obtained at the township.

Instead of saving my surplus wages, however, I took periodical excursions to Hobart Town, where I indulged in a round of dissipation, returning to my employment when the money I had drawn was exhausted.

After completing the work that was to be done, we arrived at an amicable settlement, and I resumed my journey towards the north.

Having reached the township of Brighton, I paid a visit to the local races, in the hope of meeting someone there from whom I could obtain employment. On the racecourse, however, I indulged in a drinking bout, boxing and fighting throughout the day, and at night I obtained accomodation at a hotel in Bridgewater.

At this place I renewed acquaintance with a man named Teddy Rome, who had formerly been a baker in the settlement at Port Arthur. We had some drink together, and he informed me that if I called at the house of a Mr. Stanfield I would obtain employment there. He pressed me to go that night, and although I was considerably fatigued by my frolics during the day, I at length yielded to his persuasions.

On arriving at my destination, I found that two brothers resided together in partnership, and I therefore made my application to the one who managed the business. He offered me 10/- per week, but I informed him that he would not obtain my services under 15/-, and that I was only desirous of remaining in his employment until the mowing season came on. At the same time I expressed my willingness to mow or reap with any man in the country he chose to pit against me. He appeared impressed by this assertion, and he consented to give me 15/- per week, on the understanding that the agreement was to be cancelled by either party at any time.

Three days afterwards we were hilling potatoes, and I knocked off to have a smoke. The young fellows who were working with me expressed some reluctance to follow my example, whereupon I replied htat as I was in charge of them, they could do so with no danger of incurring their master's displeasure.

Being in high spirits at the time I commenced to sing a song accompanying it by sundry gyrations and effective Shakesperian attitudes, to the wonder and admiration of the bucolic youths.

It appeared, however, that the master had observed my actions, for when I returned to the house that evening he politely informed me that he did not require any harlequins or stage-struck maniacs about his premises, as it prevented the other men from working, so that I had better try my fortune elsewhere.

I accepted the decision with good grace, and took an immediate departure, obtaining accommodation for the night at a public-house in the township.

On the following morning, I resolved to return to Hobart Town by way of the Old Beach. Reaching a homestead where I perceived a field of corn almost ripe enough for mowing, I made inquiries as to whether I could obtain employment. I ascertained that the property belonged to a Mr. Brock, who had made his money at a bakery in Hobart Town during the more palmy days.

After some discussion, during which I descanted on my own abilities to advantage, I submitted that as it was only six weeks from Christmas, I would mow and make hay for that period at £1 per week, provided that he included wet and dry weather, and drew out an agreement containing the stipulations.

He agreed to this, and as it was Saturday evening, I drew from him £1 in advance on the security of my portmanteau, promising to commence work on the following Monday. I returned according to promise, and during the day the overseer and myself got our scythes hung to suit our reach.

On the following morning, the two of us started work together, and as the overseer had the reputation of being the best mower in the district, I felt considerable curiosity as to how my own capabilities would stand in comparison with his.

The overseer led the van, and I soon discovered that if I remained a respectable distance behind him he would not exert himself, and that the moment I spurted he would also increase his speed.

That evening I happened to be behind the stable, when I overheard Brock ask the overseer how the new man (meaning myself) had worked.

"Remarkably well," was the reply. "We each cut about two acres and twenty rods."

"That is very good," returned Mr. Brock, in a pleased tone of voice, "considering the crop averages two tons to the acre."

We resumed mowing next day, with a slight increase on the result, cutting about thirty rods more than on the previous day.

On the third day Mr. Brock's son wanted to secure my position and follow the overseer, to which I raised objections, and he then put down his scythe and assumed a fighting attitude. I immediately knocked him down, and the noise of the encounter attracted the attention of the master, who, on hearing the cause of the disturbance, ordered his son to resume his original position .

Considering that young Brock overestimated his skill with the scythe, I subsequently told him that as I was the master-man I had a right to follow the overseer.

"Very well," he replied; "I will give you the belt!"

As I imagined by his reply that they had not a due knowledge of my prowess as a mower, I then challenged the overseer to cut any quantity with me, staking £6 to his £2, but he refused to make the test.

The cook employed at this place was a Frenchman, who used to cook for the old gentleman, his son, and myself. They, however, lived on the fat of the land, feasting their appetites on tasty meats, baked potatoes, and juicy vegetables; whilst for my dinner the cook invariably kneaded a quantity of flour, which he formed into the shape of fritters, and served up greasy and half-cooked on a large plate.

My epicurean tastes revolted at the coarseness of this dish, and my robust frame grew feeble for lack of more substantial diet. Therefore, I impressed a gentle hint upon him that, if he did not effect a speedy change, I would adminster a remedy that would repay him for inferior victuals and bad cooking.

The day succeeding this reminder he appeared at dinner time with the same polished bow, the same oily smile, and the same plate filled with indigestible fritters, in his hand. This was too much.

Hopefully I had looked forward through the morning to an appetising meal, and the doughy compound—accompanied as it was through the door by the savoury fumes from the master's table—lent to the pangs of hunger renewed torture.

No man with a week's longing for a "square" meal could withstand such an insult.

I seized the plate of fritters in the palm of my hand, and threw them, chinaware and all, at the cook's head.

Either the force I had infused into my aim, or the heaviness of the dough, sent the Frenchman sprawling on the floor, where he lay kicking up his heels and screaming for assistance.

The master came rushing in only to add fuel to my fiery passion, for through the half-open door came fragrant odours of the dinner, and he bore traces of its succulence on his pointed chin.

"What is the matter?" he stammered through his partly filled mouth.

"Matter!" I thundered forth, pointing at the lumps of dough. "Do you expect a man to work and live on that stuff while you wax fat on luxuries?"

He held up his hands as if utterly astounded at my expressions of discontent.

"What is it you require, then?" he enquired, with anxious voice.

"Baked meat and potatoes!" I replied, "or else dismiss the cook. If fritters satisfy frogeaters, they will not satisfy me."

The master would not dismiss the cook; neither would he permit me more substantial food, so I signified my intention of leaving at once, and demanded £2 for my ten days work at mowing. He strove to persuade me to remain, remarking that I would place him at great inconvenience; but I would not alter my resolution. After a little argument I also obtained my discharge, and, leaving the Old Beach behind me, proceeded to the watchhouse keeper at Brighton in order to notify my change of residence, in conformity with the regulations under which I retained possession of my ticket-of-leave.

CHAPTER XXI.

**Mowing and Reaping—An Indian Cowboy in Disguise—
I turn a Fortune Teller—Frisky Lasses—My Master
· Dissatisfied—From Bothwell to Launceston.**

Having acquainted the watch-house keeper at Brighton
of my change of residence I secured accomodation at a
neighbouring public-house. Next day a Mr. Findlay, who
lived near the township, entered in quest of mowers, and
I engaged with him at five shillings an acre, for mowing
and making up.

Here I remained eight days, cutting two acres daily
before dinner, and making it up in the afternoon, thus
doing a very heavy day's work. My prowess gained for
me some notoriety in this quarter, and I became known
as "Newmarket Jack, the mowing machine."

On leaving this place, I secured my discharge and also
the necessary pass permitting me to proceed on to Green
Ponds. Arriving at this township I was accosted by
Mr. Milne, coach proprietor, outside Pickering's public-
house, who informed me that a Mr. Kemp, residing three
miles away, at a place called Mount Vernon, wanted mowing hands.

I proceeded thither, and was engaged at the same rate
as I received at my last place, earning £6 for twelve
days' work.

Feeling an inclination at this time to spend a short holi-
day in Hobart Town, I procured a six days' pass on leave
from the superintendent of police for the district, at the
expiration of which I re-entered Mr. Kemp's employ,
reaping for him at ten shillings an acre. For twenty-
eight days I reaped an acre daily, so that, as my earnings
amounted to £14, I was comparatively flush of money.

I next journeyed to Spring Hill, a few miles further
on, where I was again successful in obtaining employment
at reaping. As the crop was much heavier on this land,
I received fifteen shillings per acre, and almost completed an acre daily.

When the harvest was over, I made my way to Oatlands, and had a few weeks dissipation on the strength
of my large earnings.

Growing weary of this indulgence, I went once more
in search of work, and obtained a job at laying the founda-
tion of a new house that was to be built.

This task completed, I started for Bothwell, and after
crossing the creek, paid a visit to the house of a person
whom I shall call Mr. Jones, formerly a hotel-keeper.

This gentleman was in bed at the time, but on seeing
his wife I inquired if she could provide me with accomodation for the night.

I had a portmanteau slung on each shoulder—one in
front and one at my back—and, perceiving that I was a

traveller, she inquired the nature of my business or occupation.

"I am searching for employment, madam," I replied, "but I may also inform you that I am the second celebrated Wizard of the North. With the assistance of the charts I carry in my portmanteaux, I can reveal your past and foretell your future, which I trust I may have an early opportunity of doing."

The curiosity of her sex was aroused, aind, inviting me into the kitchen, she instructed the servant to place some refreshment before me, an action which caused me intense gratification.

The mistress then expressed a desire to hear some of the mysteries I could unfold. I was in a dilemma, as I knew very little indeed relative to the social life of the good lady .

I was, however, in possession of a few facts concerning a fractious horse they had purchased, and I resolved to make use of this information to the best advantage. I begged that she would excuse me from initiating her into the mysteries of the "black art" that evening, assuring her however, that I would be highly delighted to do so on some future occasion. Then, by the exercise of a little conversational tact, I made some inquiries with reference to the fractious horse: and, owing to the interest she evinced in the matter, I extricated myself from my difficulty, for she did not refer again to fortune-telling during the remainder of the evening.

They had purchased the horse I have alluded to from a horse doctor. It was a valuable animal, but had not been properly broken in. Several persons skilled in the management of horses had endeavoured to remedy this drawback, but without success, and on one occasion the animal had almost caused the death of Mrs. Jones's nephew.

I informed Mrs. Jones that if she were willing to engage me at thirty shillings a week, I would undertake in one month to break it in so that a child might ride it.

She stated that she would have to confer with her husband on the subject, and that, as her nephew was away from home, I could occupy his room and have a conversation with Mr. Jones in the morning, an offer which I gladly accepted.

Some argument ensued between the master of the house and myself on the following day, and I finally undertook, in consideration of receiving thirty shillings per week, to have the horse under perfect control in a fortnight. I, however, achieved success in ten days, and the horse was rendered tractable enough to place in the hands of a child.

The servant girl informed me one evening, subsequent to the accomplishment of this feat, that she had heard her master and mistress commending me for being a clever, useful person, and expressing satisfaction at the agreement they had entered into with me.

Having formed a project to increase my slender means, I had some further conversation with the servant girl on general matters.

"I can read something in your eye," I at length observed with an air of mystery.

"Read away then," she replied, coquettishly.

"You are in love with your mistress's nephew," I whispered.

At this revelation she blushed with maiden modesty, and then mustered up sufficient self-possession to appear indignant at my soft impeachment

But she did not strive to conceal her amazement when I told her that the daughter of the mistress was in love with a rich doctor, and sundry other secrets the two girls fondly imagined were known to none but themselves.

I then convinced her that I had studied planets, stars, and constellations since my childhood, and that I could read their mysteries more plainly than an open book.

My object was effected, for on the following day the daughter came to me, and asked me how much I would charge to reveal her past and future

"The usual fee is £20," I replied; "but in your case I will reduce it by one half, on condition that you promise not to divulge the secret."

She accepted these terms, but told me to wait until next Oatlands market day, when her mother would be away and we would have no fear of interruption

When the eventful day arrived, the daughter came to me and presented me with five pounds, stating that it was all she had at the time, but that she would write to her brother for the other five, and give it me on its receipt.

After having locked the servant girl in the sitting-room, so that she should not interfere with me in any way, I led the daughter into another apartment.

Spreading out my charts, I perused them with all the apparent wisdom and mystery surrounding a necromancer, and then informed her of many incidents that had occurred in her past life, of the aspirations she had concealed within her bosom, after which I electrified her by prophesying what would occur during her future existence

To enable the reader to understand how I succeeded in producing this effect, I must inform him that I had discovered that the daughter and the servant girl slept together, and in order to gain the knowledge I required, I had been in the habit of placing a ladder outside their chamber after they had retired of an evening, from whence I could hear distinctly. The conversation generally carried on between the girls informed me all that I required to learn, although at times a more modest man than myself would have been put to the blush

The daughter appeared quite pleased with the replies I made to her questions, and over a bottle of elderberry wine I gave her some guidance whereby she might reach her future prospects I had shown her On one point

alone, concerning the doctor with whom she was in love,
I would not satisfy her until I had received the remaining five pounds

On liberating the servant girl, she exhibited a fresh
outburst of curiosity and impatience to be brought under
my influence She had only a £1 note, but promised to
pay me the balance of my fee when she received her
wages

I refused to open my charts until I had received
£2/10/-, whereupon she became very angry, and
threatened to inform the mistress when she returned from
market about the five pounds and the bottle of elderberry
wine the daughter had given me

On the following day the girls were running backwards and forwards from the house to the garden in
which I was working, for the purpose of asking me nonsensical questions, believing that I possessed the magic
power to answer them

The master perceived their actions, and at last grew
greatly irritated Approaching me, he said —

"Have those girls gone mad, or have you taken leave
of your senses? I am very much dissatisfied with your
conduct," he added, "and hope that I shall see no more
of it "

"If you are annoyed at what you have seen," I replied,
"you had better discharge me, for owing to a certain
reason those girls will not allow me any further peace
so long as I remain here They are both too frolicsome
and frisky, and if you were not in your dotage you would
see the same thing yourself Take my advice, give your
daughter her fortune in cash, dismiss the servant, and
let them go with me "

He would not adopt my suggestion, but endeavoured to
talk me over relative to my conduct But I persisted in
being paid my wages (£3), and he at length satisfied my
demand, when I took my departure and soon left the
frisky girls far behind me.

I proceeded to Bothwell, and put up at an hotel, the
landlady of which was a well-educated woman, but one
who had met with misfortune in her younger days

Having told her that I was a fortune-teller, she consented, as her husband was away from home, to become
a patron, and my efforts were so successful that I was
well rewarded

I was well treated at this hostelry, where I remained
a few days enjoying myself.

I then decided to proceed to Launceston, where I arrived for the first time in 1860

· CHAPTER XXII

A Bad Paymaster—Effective Reputation—Harvesting in
the North—A Pair of Idlers—Detained in Hospital
—A Troublesome Leg—An Imperial Invalid—Con-
valascent.

Harvesting season was drawing on apace when I arrived in Launceston, for I had undertaken several small
contracts on my journey

I secured suitable accommodation, and on searching
for employment was referred by a cabman to the driver
of the Deloraine coach

He conveyed me to the residence of a Mr Poole of
that township, but as that gentleman had engaged a man
during the interval, he had no need of my services In
accordance, however, with an agreement I had entered
into with the coachman, I claimed a week's wages to
liquidate my expenses, which amount was handed me
without much argument

My next engagement was with a publican who required
a groom The engagement was only of a temporary
nature, as I expressed my intention to go harvesting when
the season commenced

He did not command my services for more than a week,
however, for when that time expired, he made an excuse
for not paying me by saying that he had no change in
the house

As he had the reputation of being a bad paymaster, I
persisted in having my due, and continued obstinancy
on his part resulted in my giving him a powerful blow,
which made an incision in his cheek

His wife came to the rescue with a poker, but I parried
the blow which she made at me, and gave her a push
which sent her sprawling on the top of her prostrate husband

Having left them in this position in the bar parlour,
I made my way to the police station, and informed the
officer in charge of the occurrence

He instructed a constable to return with me, for the
purpose of advising the landlord to pay me my just dues

This policeman was an official with whom I was acquainted. He knew my passionate character, and on
reaching the public-house, he assured the landlord that
he had escaped very luckily

This statement produced such an effect upon the landlord that he immediately found the necessary change, and
he furthermore treated the constable and myself to our
choice of drink, shaking hands with us in such a friendly
manner on our departure that I felt some pangs of regret
at having dealt so hastily with him

My next journey was in the direction of the White Hills, and when I arrived at Westbury I made a stoppage at a hotel for refreshment.

Whilst I was thus recruiting myself, a young man entered with a scythe and bundle on his shoulder, who informed me that he was seeking for work at mowing.

I stated that I was bent on the same mission, and we eventually agreed to join company.

The following morning we made Longford on our way to the White Hills. I then went on the spree for five days, but my fellow-traveller succeeded in obtaining a couple of days employment at five shillings per day.

We pushed on our journey, spending one night at Evandale.

In the vicinity of the White Hills and the Sugar Loaf, we found that harvesting operations were at a standstill, owing to the unpropitious weather which prevailed at the time.

On reaching the Sugar Loaf, we waited on a Mr. Henry Gee, who rented 150 acres of land about a mile from the Cocked Hat at Breadalbane. This land bore crops ready for reaping and mowing, and which only awaited suitable weather for operations to commence.

Te occupier informed us that he had two men engaged cutting thistles at one shilling per day; but as we professed to be good harvesters, he would discharge them and give us the mowing to do; so long as we were willing to cut thistles whilst the unseasonable weather lasted.

When we commenced mowing, I discovered that my companion was inclined to be dilatory. He found too much enjoyment in his pipe, and these continual fits of laziness somewhat hampered my progress, I decided to place him on his own merits on a different portion of the ground, and pay him according to the amount of work he completed.

I then engaged a man at the rate of 15/- per week, to make up the hay which I mowed. He had been on the tramp, and so I raised no complaint against the amount of labour he did on the first day. His work, however, showed no subsequent improvement, and despite my encouragement and advice, he persisted in passing his time in the company of the young man in hte adjoining patch.

At length my words ended in blows, to which he appeared to pay more regard, but on the following morning he was missing, and also the young fellow in whose company I had travelled.

In consequence of this escapade, I was compelled to proceed to the township in order to fill the vacancies, and I also took advantage of the opportunity to procure a supply of fresh water, as that on the farm was very brackish.

I succeeded in obtaining two other hands, and in less than three months completed the work to the entire satisfaction of my employer.

Mr. Cameron, the owner of the land I had worked on for Mr. Gee, offered to lease me twenty-four acres at 10/-

per acre on the completion of my labours, giving me the use of one of his own horses and another belonging to Mr. Gee, to assist me in ploughing the land.

Mr. Gee advised me to accept the offer, stating that as I was an expert workman I would soon acquire prosperity, more especially if I entered into a matrimonial alliance. He further suggested that I should erect a rough cottage on the land, and, in consideration of my having been a Cheap Jack in England, promised to lend me a chaise cart and horse, so that I might go hawking during the slack seasons.

Instead of accepting these rosy offers to improve my position in life, I regret to state that I went on the spree for several weeks, drinking, fighting, and spending my hard-earned money until it was almost exhausted.

During this prolonged bout, I joined company with three noted fighting men, and in a severe scuffle between them my left anyle was severely injured once more.

Notwithstanding the pain occasioned thereby, I accepted the contract of thrashing the crop of a Mr. Alexander Stewart, on a farm in close proximity to the Cocked Hat.

After six weeks labour, however, my ankle became so painful that I was compelled to relinquish my task, and to obtain an order of admittance to the Launceston General Hospital.

As an inmate of that institution, Dr. Miller, the then surgeon-superintendent, did all his skill could possibly suggest to alleviate the pain and reduce the swelling, but without avail. The slightest movement on my part caused the ankle to swell enormously and increased the pain. Indeed, so serious was my condition that I was confined in the Hospital between five and six months, at the expiration of which time the last state was worse than the first, for my leg gradually broke out in small ulcerated sores.

Considering that Dr. Miller did not possess sufficient skill to combat my disease, I succeeded after some difficulty in obtaining a transfer to Hobart Town, the Hospital at the capital being then under the supervision of Dr. Smart. That gentleman, after healing the ulcers, strapped my leg from the ankle to the kneecap, and instructed me on being discharged to allow it to remain under that treatment for a period of three months, being convinced that this course would prevent further swelling.

At the time of my admission, the Hobart Town Hospital was in a very crowded state, which accounts for the reason of my discharge.

The surgeon-superintendent held a consultation with the honorary medical officers, the upshot being that I was sent to Port Arthur as an imperial invalid, with strict injunctions regarding the treatment of my leg. If the doctors opinion was confirmed at the expiration of three months I was to be returned to Hobart Town, and placed in a position to obtain my own livelihood.

Three months passed away, and the strapping was removed. Unfortunately, however, this caused the leg to assume its old condition, whilst the pain was excrutiating.

My life was a burden to me. Never previously had I more regretted my youthful follies and excesses, which had practically given birth to the miserable condition I was then in.

Taverns and the haunts of ill-repute, spit of all watchfulness and self-control, have proved a continual source of wretchedness and suffering to me from that time until the present.

May this acknowledgment, and the expression of my sincere repentance, warn those who, reading this book, are as yet but striplings amidst the terrible dangers and temptations which beset existence.

Weeks of indescribable agony rolled slowly over my head. Unable to move—unable to obtain the slightest relief from pain—that brief interval in its agony counterbalanced all the misery and oppression I had passed through in the days which were behind. The slightest movement of my leg caused the ulcers to renew their insidious attacks with twofold vigour, and the limb increased in size daily.

My condition improved somewhat between 1861 and 1871, and I made several journeys between Port Arthur and Hobart Town with the object of improving my condition in life, but I was at last compelled to relinquish that attempt

I then had serious thoughts of having the diseased limb amputated, and indeed left Port Arthur for the capital on occasion with that object in view But when I waited on the house surgeon of the Hospital he exhibited some reluctance to perform the operation, and suggested that as Dr Smart had been my first medical adviser in Hobart Town I should await his return from Fingal, when he would consult with that gentleman He experssed some doubts as to the advisableness of having the leg amputated at the time, dreading that it would be accompanied by fatal effects

"If it be God's will," I replied, "I will bow to it with resignation. Better death than lifelong misery."

When the consultation was held the medical gentlemen declined to undertake the responsibility of the operation. This was in one sense an extremely fortunate decision for me, as shortly afterwards my leg improved so rapidly that I determined on leaving the capital and revisiting Launceston.

CHAPTER XXIII.

An Unlucky Acquaintance—The Butchers' Arms—A Fracas with a Drunkard—Under Arrest—Death of Hunt —The Inquest—A Daughter of Erin—Indicted for Wilful Murder—Perplexities and Misfortunes.

Early on the morning I had decided to start on my journey to Launceston, I proceeded to a wholesale establishment in Murray Street, kept by a Mr. Bealey, for the purpose of purchasing a stock of provisions to carry me on my journey.

As I was crossing the intersection of Murray Street with Liverpool Street, I was accosted by a man who inquired the whereabouts of the Butchers' Arms public-house.

I gave him the necessary directions; but as he was under the influence of liquor, he was unable to understand me, and, producing a bag of money, he stated that if I escorted him thither, he would recoup me for my trouble.

After much persuasion on his part, and his assurance that the landlord and his wife were old shipmates whom he had not seen for a length of time, I consented to accompany him; but I experienced considerable difficulty in conducting him to his destination, for his gait was none of the steadiest.

The host and hostess, who addressed him by the name of Martin, appeared delighted to renew the acquaintanceship of the stranger, who immediately ordered breakfast for me and also half a gallon of ale and a pint of gin. I, however, preferred bottled porter and bread and cheese, and whilst I was discussing this refreshment, Martin tendered me half a crown for my services.

The morning wore away and my newly-found friend continued to call for beer and spirits for the benefit of those who were congregated in the bar.

A cordial invitation to remain to dinner was extended to me by the landlord, which I accepted. Before that repast was ready, however, a man by the name of James Hunt, a bricklayer's labourer, entered the bar, and perceiving the flowing tankards which had been provided by the liberality of Martin, he helped himself to two pots of beer in succession.

It was whilst he was quaffing the last of these that I walked into the taproom from the parlour, from whence I had been an eye-witness of his movements. Immediately he perceived my entrance, he placed himself in an attitude of defiance, and commenced hurling insults upon me, chief among which was the epithet of being a "flagellating dog." My compassion was aroused by his miserable attire and degraded appearance, and, despite the promptings of my passion, I maintained sufficient control over myself to treat his remarks with forbearance.

Failing to arouse my ire, he devoted his attention to

the landlord, making liberal use of maledictions and threats.

Here, again, his conduct evoked the well-merited contempt it deserved; but he was so inflamed by drink that the small remnants of self-respect and shame he possessed had temporarily fled from him.

Repulsed by the landlord, he stepped over to where I was sitting, and commanded me to stand up, otherwise he would strike me as I sat. His threatening attitude was not to be lightly disregarded; therefore, I arose and stood prepared to defend myself from any drunken freak. He made a desperate lunge at me; but stepping nimbly aside I avoided the blow, aind he fell a shapeless mass upon the floor.

Deeming it high time that he should be ejected, I caught him by the collar with that object in view and dragged him to the door, but perceivnig a constable coming that way on his beat, I told the man to sit down in the bar, as I did not desire to have him locked up. He complied with my advice, and I took up a position in an opposite corner.

The man remained peaceable enough until a big swaggering fellow known as "Yorkey" entered the bar, and sympathised with Hunt. Presently he jumped to his feet, and addressing Hunt, said—"Tha' an' me will give the old flagellator a good beating."

The spirits of the crestfallen man revived, and he was not slow to respond to the invitation of the Yorkshireman.

They assumed the aggressive, and as Hunt was the foremost, I gave him a blow which sent him across the bar into a passage leading to the kitchen.

"Yorkey," on seeing his companion treated in this manner, at once turned round and beat an undignified retreat.

I then endeavoured to get my arms underneath Hunt in order to carry out my former purpose of ejecting him; but at that moment the landlady came to me, and placing her hand on my shoulder, persuaded me to interfere no further with the prostrate man.

She further begged of me to go into the kitchen, as dinner was ready, but although she prevailed upon me to do so, I was unable to eat anything, as my temper was considerably aroused at having been called a "flagellating dog" without just reason, and I was anxious to go into the bar and give him as much as he deserved.

"For my sake, do nothing of the kind," said Mrs. Bryant. "Why not meet the man when he is sober, and speak to him of his conduct.'

"Speak to him!" I cried. "Do you not think I have received sufficient insults to justify me in administering more summary chastisement to the man?"

"You have, indeed," she returned, "but pray do not return to the bar, for I am told that you are such a passionate man, and may probably overstep the bounds of prudence. Go by the back gate and I will give you five shillings to enjoy yourself elsewhere "

After some further persuasion on her part, I took her advice, and left the house by the back gate, proceeding to my home after having a glass, for the sake of "auld lang syne," with a couple of gay women I was acquainted with, one of whom, seeing my lame condition, pressed a half-sovereign upon me.

On the following morning I returned to the Butchers' Arms, and made inquiries for the stranger named Martin, whom I had met on the previous day

"Oh, he has returned to his work at the Old Beach," said Mr Bryant "He got drinking and fighting yesterday' and managed to lose what money, he did not spend "

"And has Hunt not paid a visit to you this morning?" I inquired

"He only left the house a short time ago," Mr. Bryant answered "He said that he was suffering from an internal injury and was going to the Hospital for treatment "

"What brought him here this morning?" I queried

"Why man, he did not leave here last night,' was the reply "About eight or nine o'clock I put him into the stable to sleep, and before I retired for the night, went to see if everything was safe in the yard, when I found Hunt walking about, apparently in great pain. I gave him a glass of gin and another one this morning, and as his condition appeared to become gradually worse, he decided to go to the Hospital "

After a little further conversation with the landlord I left the house, and when passing by the Sir John Franklin public-house, a friend invited me inside to have a glass of drink with him

Whilst chatting together over our refreshments, my arms were suddenly pinioned from behind, and turning my head I perceived that three constables had charge of me

"You have knocked a man's eye out and done something serious this time," said one of them.

For the purpose of identification, I was taken to the Hospital, where Hunt declared me to be the man who had knocked him down and kicked him

The injured man expired after a week's illness, the doctor certifying that death was due to internal rupture.

An inquest on the body was held on the following day, when I, of course, was present in custody

Mr. Bryant (the landlord of the Butchers' Arms public-house) stated in his evidence that Hunt had placed himself before me in fighting attitude, loudly proclaiming what he would do to me and calling me an old flagellating dog When I arose from my seat, Hunt had fallen to the floor, and I then dragged him to the door and left him there uninjured He (the landlord) left the bar about this time, and could not therefore swear as to what finally occurred between us.

Mrs Bryant was the next witness, and she gave evidence to the effect that about ten minutes after she had relieved her husband in the bar, she saw me knock Hunt down and stamp on his abdomen

This statement intensified the delicacy of my position, and one could almost read on the faces of those present the impression which it made.

The next person called was an old Irishwoman Her sworn statement was that she had been in the bar of the public-house referred to, and she had seen me knock Hunt down and stamp on his "chist'

The Coroner "'Was it not the abdomen that he stamped on, my good woman?"

Witness : "An' phat is that, yer Wusshup?"

The Coroner· "Why, the belly to be sure "

Witness "Faix, an' shure it wus, yer Wusshup "

At this stage I intervened, and asked the Coroner why he had not explained to the witness that the abdomen was the big toe, as the woman would probably have made a similar reply.   I protested against him putting such words into the mouths of witnesses as tended to criminate me

The Coroner "Make no remarks If you do not remain quiet, I will have you removed"

Upon this, I vented a passionate outburst upon him, during which I told him that the jurisdiction he dispensed appeared to be of a very tyrannical and one-sided nature

When I had concluded, he did not carry out his threat to have me removed, and, as I remained silent after that, the case was proceeded with

The remaining evidence was of little interest, chiefly having reference to Hunt's statements and my identification

The jury returned a verdict in accordance with the medical testimony, adding that the injuries had been sustained through the abdomen having been stamped on by me   They, therefore, recorded a verdict of manslaughter, and I was conveyed to gaol to await my trial at the next Criminal Sessions of the Supreme Court.

The following morning one of the newspapers committed a breach of journalistic etiquette by commenting on the case sub judice, and the article was most injurious to me It stated, among other comments, that the coroner had very little doubt in his mind that the Attorney-General—the grand jury of this colony—would indict me for wilful murder, referring by way of comparison to a case of a similar nature which had occurred in England, where a schoolmaster had knocked a boy down and stamped on his abdomen, causing his death

Why the newspaper cited the statement of the coroner and the incident referred to, I cannot imagine, and more especially the latter, as it was irrelevant to my case The Attorney-General, however, did not file a bill of wilful murder against me

The danger of my position was increased by the fact that I had no money to procure council, nor had any advocate been retained by the Crown on my behalf.

When the visiting clergyman came to see me, I requested him to procure me the depositions made at the inquest, that I might be better enabled to defend myself. He, however, would not comply, on the grounds that I would receive an impartial trial.

My indignation was great indeed at being thus defied and rebuked on every side. I was to stand my trial on a capital offence; my life was in imminent danger; and I was not permitted to prepare my own defence. From the conflicting evidence given at the inquest, I felt convinced that a lawyer on my behalf would have had a good case to work upon. But this legal luxury was denied me, nor could I by any means obtain the depositions, and become more conversant with the discrepancies of the witnesses.

No man placed in the same position as I was, when Hunt and "Yorkey" so unprovokedly insulted and assaulted me, would have listened calmly and borne chastisement with folded arms. The blow with which I felled Hunt was given in self-defence; the force of it was due to the ungovernable temper he had aroused within me, but I had no desire or intention to inflict severe injury upon him.

My sorrow on hearing of his death was sincere and heartfelt. Never previously had I so much moaned in secret over the fruits of my vitiated habits and evil passions; and these feelings were intensified by the knowledge I obtained that Hunt had gone to his doom without seeking pardon for an ill-spent life, but carrying with him a multitude of sins to answer for.

CHAPTER XXIV

My Trial for Murder—"Guilty of Manslaughter"—A Second Life Sentence—Port Arthur Again—A Horrible Life—In Hospital—A Clever Cook— Treachery—An Unjust Accusation—Back to the Prison Walls.

On the 13th day of February, 1872, I was arraigned at the Supreme Court, Hobart Town, for the wilful murder of James Hunt

Although under the impression that it is a recognised procedure in English Courts for the judge to appoint a lawyer to watch the case on behalf of an undefended prisoner charged with a capital offence, the Crown did not even at the last moment provide me with counsel, and I therefore had to conduct my own defence

The evidence of Mr and Mrs Bryant corroborated that given by them at the inquest, but the Irishwoman had not been subpœned, the Crown Prosecutor being probably under the impression that her evidence would not stand the ordeal of cross-examination

After the doctor had been examined as to the cause of Hunt's death, I asked him if the rupture could not have been caused by other means than a stamp on the abdomen.

"Yes," he replied, "a fall—and even a slight fall—may cause internal rupture when a man is besotted with drink."

"Were there any prints on the abdomen of the deceased man," I inquired, "to indicate that he had been stamped upon'

"No," he replied, "there was no mark of violence upon the body, but the abdomen is likely to give way to a stamp without leaving any impression"

The judge then asked the doctor how long it would be before the pain would originate after a rupture had been caused

"About ten minutes," was the answer

Mrs Bryant, who had not left the court room, was then recalled, and stated that Hunt complained of being in pain about ten minutes after I had knocked him down and stamped on him

In addressing the jury, I stated that the only evidence they had before them on which they could possibly convict me was the unsupported testimony of Mrs. Bryant, and asked why the other woman who gave evidence at the inquest had not been produced. I pointed out that the doctor had stated in his evidence that the rupture might have been caused by a fall, however slight Was it not possible, then, that Hunt had caused the injury when he first fell on the floor, according to the statement of Mr Bryant, after having made a futile blow at me? I submitted that the landlady was not in a position to assert that Hunt had complained of pain ten minutes after my alleged ill-treatment, for she had been in my company in the kitchen for some time after the occurrence, persuading me to leave the house before I used undue violence towards the man Mr Bryant had stated that he had not noticed Hunt in pain until ten or eleven o'clock at night, when he gave him a glass of gin, therefore, I submitted that these two facts overthrew the evidence of Mrs Bryant, who had been illegally in court at the time the doctor had given his evidence and was willing to swear anything that would save her from having the license of the public-house cancelled, or from a second prosecution for keeping a disorderly house I impressed upon the jury that Hunt was in a miserable and ragged state at the time of the dispute, that he had been drinking heavily for weeks at the lowest public-houses, and I contended—waiving the evidence of Mrs Bryant—that it was quite possible he had either sustained the injury before he entered the house, or between the hour of my departure in the morning and the time Mr. Bryant had first found him suffering from pain in the evening The evidence of Mrs Bryant was all they had to go upon, and I affirmed, in conclusion, that if it were considered dispassionately, it would be found at utter variance with the facts I had substantiated Why I should be charged with wilful murder I could not conceive. It had been shown clearly that the blow I made at Hunt was in self defence, that there was no premeditation on my part; and I left it to the jury to form an unbiassed opinion as to whether I had kicked Hunt, as alleged

My address lasted a considerable time, but it failed to convince the "good men and true" of my entire innocence, for they returned into court with the verdict "Guilty of manslaughter," and for the second time, I received a life sentence.

Shortly afterwards I was sent to Port Arthur to undergo the term, and was once more placed in the Model Prison

When I arrived, however, I was suffering such intense agony from the pain of my ulcerated leg that I was unable to walk, and had to be carried to my cell Nor had I sufficient power to sling my hammock, so was compelled to lie on the cold bare floor all night

On the following morning I complained to the doctor of my condition, and on examining the leg, he ordered some treatment, but abruptly refused my request to be provided with a mattress instead of the hammock.

The commandant at this time was Mr H Boyd, and when he came round I informed him of the doctor's harshness towards me, whereupon he said that although he could not interfere with the doctor's decision he would order that my hammock should be slung for me every evening

"Thank you sir, for your kindness," I replied, "but I shall not derive any benefit thereby, as the pain of my leg will not permit me to lie in the hammock"

"I know you must be in great pain," he said, "for I heard you groaning on the voyage down last evening. I sympathise with you, but I am sorry to say I cannot countermand the doctor's orders "

Fortunately for me the officer who was in charge of the Model Prison (Mr Townley, son of a former schoolmaster at Norfolk Island) was a very humane man He saw the misery and pain I bore and took compassion upon me, and a few days afterwards, when accompanying the doctor on his rounds, he begged that official to allow me a mattress, stating that it was painful to hear me groaning day and night, and to see me continually lying on the bare boards   The doctor gave the necessary permission, but evidently with a bad grace, and the mattress was sent to me almost immediately.

After two or three months constant rest, the leg healed up, and the pain ceased

Utterly weary of being idle and confined to my cell, I easily obtained consent from the doctor and the commandant to make fancy grass brooms for the use of the institution, the latter giving instructions that I should be regularly supplied with the material

The commandant exhibited much pleasure at the first broom I made, and promised that if I continued to make others equally good, he would do what he could for my benefit

I remained at this employment for a few months, working in a cell set apart for the purpose

At length, however, my leg exhibited symptons of returning to its former diseased condition. When I rested quietly it would improve, but the slightest exertion caused the ulcers to break out with renewed vigour   I was compelled to see the doctor and obtain exemption from work, upon hearing which the commandant became very angry. He visited my cell, and asked me if I could not make the brooms without moving elsewhere, remarking that he was very anxious to send some of the articles to the Government institutions in Hobart Town

I assured him that it was impossible for me to do so, as I was unable to stand up, whereupon he left me in a very bad humour

Twelve months of my sentence expired without anything of further interest transpiring, and I was released from the Model Prison.

I may explain that it was a rule in the case of long-sentenced prisoners to confine them in separate cells in the Model Prison for a term regulated by the length of the sentence they had to undergo, and, as I was a life prisoner, I was confined in these gloomy precincts for twelve months.

So long as I was treated in conformity with the prison regulations, without undue harshness being exercised, I had resolved to conform to obedience and discipline, and I had little cause for complaint so far as the Model Prison was concerned

The first order I received on being discharged from that institution was to break up a heap of metal. Although suffering extreme pain, I performed my task on the first day without complaining, but on the second day I was compelled to inform the doctor of my inability to continue the work.

He refused in a rough manner to exempt me, and I passed the remainder of the day in great misery.

On the following morning I received the same reply to my request for exemption, and I then told the doctor he was a most brutal and unfeeling monster for exercising oppression upon a helpless being such as I was, instead of faithfully discharging his proper duty.

Upon this he instructed a constable to lead me away to the stone heap. That individual expressed much sympathy for me, and also his regret that it was not in his power to aid me in some way.

I told him in confidence that there was a limit to human forbearance, and that as it was a very small one in my case, I would commit some rash act if they continued to make me the object of their tyranny.

Two or three days afterwards, I requested the muster-master to allow me to fall out and see the doctor again, and he ordered me into the yard until he had done mustering the men. As soon as he had completed that duty he sent for me, and threatened to lock me up if I did not go immediately to the stone heap, and that on no plea would he allow me to see the doctor.

I started work accordingly, but as the muster-master was compelled to pass by me on returning to his house for breakfast, I resolved to attack him with a long knife I had concealed in my possession.

When he passed by, nearly opposite to where I was standing, I jumped up in a violent passion and made towards him, without, however, exposing the knife.

He was an awful coward, for when he saw the determination with which I approached him, he hastened to assure me that I need not break any stones, but sit down or walk about if I chose to do so. He promised to screen me from any trouble, so long as I remained near my heap.

Content with these assurances, I thanked him and walked back to my heap, on which I sat for the remainder of the day.

Next morning I kept my bed and persisted in my application to see the doctor. The officer (Mr. Morley) in charge of the division I was in, kindly spoke to the doctor on my behalf, and his statements secured me entire exemption from work.

My clergyman (the Rev. Rr. Haywood, a gentleman for whom I entertained sincere respect) subsequently visited me, and through his intercession I was admitted into the Hospital, the medical gentleman in charge being very kind to me and attentive in his treatment.

In consequence of overhearing the patients continually cursing and grumbling because the cook was in the habit of curtailing the allowance of food, and at the bony nature of the meat, I thought I would try to remedy the evil by writing a statement on the slate to the doctor, stating what proportion of meat per pound would be actually wasted in the cooking, a problem I had long since solved

When the doctor came round on the following day, I referred him to the slate, which stated that the cooks deducted 6oz instead of 4oz per lb for waste He remarked that my remedy was worth looking into, and advised me to lay the matter before the commandant

I did so, and the result was that I was appointed to the Hospital cookhouse, and at my request the other cook was given outside employment

On the first day I turned out 12oz of meat to the pound, and my cooking gave the men such entire satisfaction that when the Rev Mr Haywood visited the ward several of them told him that they had never previously had such excellent soup, nor such a liberal allowance of meat   The reverend gentleman took an opportunity before leaving to express his pleasure at my success, and congratulated me on the good opinion I had gained

A few days after this incident, I asked the prisoner cook whom I had deposed to take my pint of soup to my ward. He did so, and in the course of a few minutes I went to my ward and drank the soup, which had been placed in a quart dish

Immediately, I felt a burning sensation in my throat, but on making inquiries I found that the other men had not experienced these unpleasant symptons from the soup

My suspicions were aroused, and I discovered that the discharged cook had put croton oil into the liquid to injure me.

I reported the circumstance on the following day, but the man received no punishment, and was simply removed to a more desirable situation in the cookhouse for the insane.

When this arrangement was made known to me in the ward, I remarked that the man should have received some punishment for so serious an offence, and expressed my intention of seeing the doctor about his leniency, and also of interviewing the commandant

Before I had an opportunity of addressing the doctor when he put in an appearance on the following morning, he abruptly ordered the constable on duty to take me to the Model Prison, without stating his motive for doing so

Taken before the commandant for trial on the following morning, it transpired that a free invalid, who was messenger for the Hospital, and a couple of the patients had placed a wrong construction on the remarks I made relative to seeing the doctor about the cook's punishment, and reported that I had threatened to murder both the doctor and the commandant

In order to controvert the evidence given by the two prisoner patients in the Hospital. I requested that the constable who was on duty at the time should be placed on oath.

This was done, and this disinterested witness repeated the exact words I had made use of with regard to seeing the doctor and the commandant.

The latter official, however, was not convinced that my words had been misconstrued, and wished to send for another prisoner to give evidence.

I expressed an opinion that there was no necessity to go to so much trouble over such a trifle, and that if no reliance was to be placed on the testimony of the constable, he was not fit for the position he held.

For this I was severely censured by the commandant, and once more my temper caused me to lose control over myself and I treated the bench to a tirade of abuse.

In retaliation, the commandant sentenced me to seven days solitary confinement on bread and water, with a recommendation to the Governor-in-Council that I should be detained in the Model Prison until further orders.

CHAPTER XXV

Another Attempt at Murder—Failure and Repentance—
The Commandant and the Baker—An Official Visit
—Sir Frederick Weld—Ministerial Redress—Dead
Island—Abandonment of Port Arthur.

Brooding over this new punishment, I resolved to revenge myself on the doctor for the summary manner in which he had dealt with me

As soon as I was placed in the cell to undergo my solitary confinement, I broke the table and bookshelves into pieces, and then commenced calling out for the head warder of the prison   When he arrived, I requested him to take me to the refractory cell, as I had been guilty of fractious conduct, but he would not comply with my desire until I threatened to fracture his head on the first opportunity if he persisted in his refusal

With the assistance of another warder he then escorted me to the refractory cell, and on the following morning I asked to see the doctor

When that individual came, I had to pass through two doors leading from the cell to a third door, and on reaching that entrance I was guarded on the right hand side by a constable

In the palm of my right hand I had a knife, and this I kept concealed by placing my arm at full length down my side   With the fingers of my left hand I kept my jaws open under the pretence of having a gathering on the palate of my mouth

There were a few steps leading from the ground to the open door at which I stood, and as the doctor put his foot on, the first of these, I endeavoured to clutch the knife so that I could plunge it into his heart

Either my movement was too awkward or too hasty, for the constable by my side, being a keen-witted fellow, was attracted by the working of the arm, and he quickly demanded what I had in my hand

The head warder, who had accompanied the doctor to the cell and was awaiting him below, overheard the constable, and he shouted—

"Come down, doctor.   That man has something in his hand "

The doctor was not long in retreating, and the words were no sooner uttered than, recognising that I was baffled, I shoved the constable aside, and, hastening into my cell, secreted the knife in its former position

The head warder shouted out that if I did not hand over whatever instrument I had concealed, he would come up and knock my brains out with the constable's staff

"If you come up here," I returned, "I will serve you in the manner that I intended to serve the doctor "

They held a short consultation, and then went away. Two or three hours later, however, the head warder returned with some additional constables. They instituted a strict search of my clothing and the cell, but they did not succeed in finding the instrument which would have consigned me to firther punishment.

The next morning I bitterly repented having attempted to murder the doctor, and took an early opportunity of sending for the Rev. Mr. Hayward.

Upon that gentleman's arrival, I entrusted him with the knife, and confided to him the design I had formed.

"I did not succeed," I said, "and I am glad of it now. I really believe that the Higher Power prevented me from committing this murder; but in giving you the knife I rely upon your secrecy."

He assured me that I could repose implicit confidence in him, and accordingly I heard no more of my murderous attempt.

A short time after, the members of the Executive Council, accompanied by several gentlemen of position, paid a visit to the settlement, and on being asked if any of us desired to see the Premier or the Attorney-General, I wrote my name down as being desirous of that privilege.

The Honourable William Moore was a member of the Executive Council at that time, holding the portfolio of Minister of Lands and Works.

I informed the members of the cruelty I had undergone since my imprisonment at Port Arthur, and assured them that if they examined the books I could point out how many acts of injustice had been committed. This they did not do, but they gave me permission to return to my cell on the understanding that I was to produce something which was a disgrace to the institution.

I went and brought back one of my blankets for their inspection. Having washed one corner thoroughly clean, the contrast was so great that the filthy state of the blanket was plainly noticeable.

I next pointed out to the Ministers that a certain number of the prisoners had been employed in making fancy mats and carpets some of which were laid down in the corridors of the prison. The most expensive Government rugs had been pulled to pieces for the purpose of altering them into suitable widths and lengths, and I humbly begged that the members of the Council would be kind enough to give instructions that we should in future have clean healthy bedding, instead of fancy carpets to give the prison a palatial appearance on the arrival of visitors. These carpets, I added, were only laid down on special occasions, and were taken up immediately the strangers had departed.

The Executive as a body showed no encouragement or sympathy with me, but the Honourable William Moore subsequently came to me, and candidly admitted that he thought that there was a great deal of truth in my remarks. He was also good enough to promise that, as Governor Weld would be visiting the prison in a short time, he would mention my case to his Excellency.

For this kindness I expressed my sincere gratitude, and I may also add that in the course of a day or two we all received a supply of clean bedding

It was not long before Governor Weld arrived, and when I saw him and made my complaints he gave me a very patient hearing   He was then pleased to order my release from the Model Prison, and, at my own request, had me sent to take charge of Dead Island

Every Saturday afternoon I was taken back to the settlement, starting for the island on Monday mornings

After a time I was removed from Dead Island, and placed in a small room attached to the lumber yard, where a number of other mechanics were, at work

Mr McNaught, the overseer of the bakehouse and cookhouse, took tally of the amount of work done by the mechanics during the day

After I had been in this room, where I was exempt from labour by the new commandant, Dr Coverdale, for a few days, I complained to McNaught of the bread being of a doughy, sticky, and pasty nature, and stated that it was done for fraud, in order to make it weigh heavy, and so obtain a surplus from the pound and a half of flour allowed on each two-pound loaf   It could not be the fault of the flour, as I had, when at Dead Island, turned out first-class bread with the same article

I took my allowance to the station master, and requested him to take me to the commandant, so that I might prevail upon that gentleman to have the cause explained, but I only received a promise that I should have an interview with the commandant on Saturday night

But when that time arrived, I was again disappointed, for the commandant, it appeared, would not see anyone.

On Monday morning, when the Rev. Mr. Hayward was passing by on his way home after prayers, I went over to inform him of being unable to see the commandant, and also to tell him that as the prisoner who cleaned the church and milked the cow had been taken away from him owing to an altercation he had had with the commandant, I was willing to perform those duties, provided he could obtain the necessary leave of absence for me.

When we separated, Mr. McNaught shouted after me that he would have me arrested for leaving my work, and also for insulting him with regard to the bread

I answered that I was not employed at any work, and that I had the permission of Commandant Coverdale, who was also doctor at this time, to remain in my room and rest my leg, and to walk within the limits of the settlement if I chose to do so

Anyway, he sent for three constables and had me locked up in the Model Prison to await my trial

After he had sworn to the charges on the following day, I asked the commandant if he had not, as medical officer, exempted me from all labour, adding that the books would prove that there was no work set against my name, and that by examining both his own and

McNaught's he could easily satisfy himself that such was the case.

Instead of the commandant inspecting the books, he directed McNaught to proceed with his statement, which at once roused my temper, and I accused the commandant of being accessory to the perjury McNaught was committing, concluding with the abusive language I considered he deserved.

He ordered me to the Model Prison, stating his intention of sending my case to Hobart Town for trial. He carried this into effect, with the result that I was sentenced to fourteen days solitary confinement on bread and water. Had impartial justice been shown, McNaught would have been tried for perjury, instead of punishment being inflicted upon me.

In the early part of the year 1877, Governor Weld and the new Ministry, which included the Honourable Thomas Reibey (Premier), and the Honourable Mr. Bromby (Attorney-General), paid a periodical visit to Port Arthur for the purpose of hearing the complaints of prisoners. Those desirous of interviewing the Ministers and there was a large number on this occasion—were ranked up two deep before the office, and called in one after another.

Either by chance or otherwise, I was the last to present myself before the vice-regal party, and before I had proceeded far with my statements, his Execellency warned me to exercise discretion as to the accusations I made.

I respectfully informed his Excellency that if he would be good enough to grant me the opportunity, I could substantiate the charges of perjury I wished to make against the commandant and McNaught.

His Excellency then allowed me to proceed with my statement, and evinced so much interest in my case, that he continued writing down for the space of an hour the complaints I had to make.

I then humbly asked his Excellency to investigate my statements, and if he found them substantiated to give me redress for the cruel and unlawful treatment imposed upon me.

His Excellency signified his intention of doing so, and also promised that I should have an interview with the Premier and Attorney-General before their departure in the morning.

I had prepared details of the complaints I had to make and these I left in the hands of the authorities for presentation to the Executive Council.

The following morning the Honourable Thomas Reibey visited me in my cell, and informed me that his Excellency Sir Frederick Weld, himself, and the Attorney-General, had had a long conversation at Government House relative to my case. He assured me that his Excellency was kindly disposed towards me, as he had stated that, no matter how bad a man was, he deserved some consideration. Mr. Reibey then expressed a hope that, if the Executive sanctioned my release from the Model Prison, I would commit no indiscretion either by word or deed, as it would reflect on their action in having liberated me. He suggested that as Port Arthur would be broken up in a short time, I should return to Dead Island in the meantime, where there would be less risk of incurring trouble.

After Mr. Reibey's departure, the Attorney-General came in, and stated that he had read the complaints written by me. He had found that what I had stated therein was correct, and he promised to do all he could, in conjunction with the Premier, to induce his Excellency the Governor to grant me my liberty after they had returned to Hobart Town.

Under these cheering circumstances, I gladly accepted the Honourable Mr. Reibey's offer to proceed to Dead Island, where I remained, under the same conditions as before, until the breaking up of the settlement, during which time I succeeded in maintaining the promise I had made not to commit myself in any way.

On the 17th day of April, 1877, the major portion of the prisoners, including myself, were transferred from Port Arthur to Hobart Town, only a few remaining behind to carry out some necessary work.

CHAPTER XXVI.

Removal to Hobart Town—Troubles in the Penitentiary —Too Outspoken—De Lunatico Inquirendo—Attempts to Regain Liberty—My Present Situation.

Manifestations of curiosity were observable on every side when we arrived in Hobart Town, and crowds of people congregated on the wharfs to obtain a glimpse of us, for we had the unenviable reputation of being a desperate set of characters.

We were at once escorted to the Penitentiary in conveyances, and I was there drafted into a model department known as the "H" division, although I had committed no breach of the regulations to warrant such treatment.

In less than an hour after my allotment, the Premier (the Honourable Thomas Reibey) came to see me, and made many kind inquiries as to how I had been progressing since his visit to Port Arthur.

I informed that gentleman that I had experienced great difficulty in respecting the promise I had made him, and that I attributed my resignation to the Higher Power giving me the strength I prayed for to overcome those temptations to which my weak nature was prone. I pointed out to him the injustice of the authorities in placing me in the "H" division without just cause, more especially as my ulcerated leg was causing me extreme pain.

He expressed much sympathy towards me, and promised that he would interview his Excellency the Governor on the matter.

On the following day I informed the superintendant (Mr. Atkins) and the doctor of the promise the Premier had made me, and the first-named official denied all connection with the arrangement.

Some redress was extended towards me next morning for I was removed next to the exempt ward in a room where there were two other prisoners, but I was not thoroughly satisfied, and on the superintendent coming round I inquired why I had not been placed in the exempt ward instead of the large cold ward I was then in.

He replied that the exempt ward was full, but I remarked that it was not full of invalid patients, for there were men sleeping in it at night who were able to work during the day. I stated that it was unfair to exclude me from that department when there were men who could be removed elsewhere without entailing suffering or additional hardship upon them. I also complained to the doctor, and asked him to have me transferred to the the exempt ward left open for my benefit, and also that not under his treatment, but my request met with no practical response.

This caused me to accuse the superintendent of driving me into further misery and temptation, for my leg was so painful that I could not walk about, and the intense coldness of my room prevented me from keeping myself warm.

He promised that he would have the door leading into th eexempt ward left open for my benefit, and also that he would put a stove in my ward as soon as he could possibly manage to do so.

To give an instance of how conspicuous was the harsh treatment exhibited towards me, I may state that a gentleman came to visit the Penitentiary one day, and on meeting the superintendent, he inquired why I was not placed in the exempt ward, where I would receive proper treatment instead of being compelled to remain in cold and misery.

The reply was to the effect that I was disagreeable and continually falling out with my fellow prisoners, but at the same time he omitted to state that I was living in perfect harmony with two other men. His real object was, however, to keep me away from a large body of men, in order that I should not incite them to complain of the fraud perpetuated on their rations.

No wonder that I grew sullen and discontented by these persecutions, and felt goaded on to abuse those in authority over me.

The climax came at length when his Excellency Governor Weld visited the establishment.

In answer to his inquiry as to my condition, I complained bitterly of having been put in the "H" division, with a damp miserable yard for exercise, and a room of the separate treatment. I stated how obstinately I had been debarred from participating in the privileges of the exempt ward, and of the manner in which I was persecuted.

He interrupted me, however, and said that I had always been complaining at Port Arthur, and that I seemed determined to pursue the same line of conduct in the Penitentiary.

"I beg your Excellecy's pardon," I rejoined, "but did I not express my ability to substatniate the complaints at Port Arthur? If they had been impartially investigated, McNaught would have been convicted of perjury, and the commandant of being an accessory. You gave me no redress, however, and it is in this manner that the authorities are encouraged to treat the regulations with contempt."

His Excellency appeared annoyed, and made a gesture to command silence.

"Do you know whom you are addressing?" he inquired.

"Yes, your Excellency," I replied, "I am aware of your position, and the power you possess, and it is on this account that I appeal to you once more for that justice which I had hoped to receive long ere this."

He made some remarks which I deemed were unwarranted, and it is with sincere shame and sorrow I confess that my ungovernable passion caused me to forget the respect due to my visitor, and I made use of language which from that day I have regretted.

A few weeks subsequently, Dr. Denham, whom I had been under as an invalid at Port Arthur, came to visit me. He asked me a great number of questions relative to my past life, and especially regarding the terms on which I stood with the Rev. Mr. Haywood.

I told the doctor that my admiration for my late clergy-man had greatly decreased, as I did not coincide with the new-fangled ideas he was introducing into his religion. Moreover, I did not believe the clergyman to be a sincere Christian for he had refused to write to the Governor-in-Council on my behalf when he saw that I had not been treated according to the rules, stating as an excuse that—although he was a clergyman and a justice of the peace—the authorities would not take any notice of his complaint. But I assured the doctor that I harboured no vindictive feeling against the clergyman, and that, if it were possible, I would express to him, in some practical form, my appreciation of the kindness he had always shown me prior to the incident referred to.

This visit by the doctor must have been made as a preliminary examination into my sanity, for a short time afterwards I was taken to the superintendent's office, where he, the under-sheriff, and Dr. Turnbull were assembled in solemn conclave to inquire into my mental condition.

The first question put to me was by the under-sheriff, who inquired if I was unable to keep my temper.

"You wish me to say 'No,'" I replied, "so that I shall be considered unaccountable for my actions. But you are not responsible for my actions, for there is a Higher Power than human that rules my temper. Moreover, when it causes me to commit crime, I am justly punished for the offence, and therefore free from further punishment for the time being.

After some other question of minor importance had been put to me, the examination ceased, and the medical men consulted together for a short time, after which they came to the unanimous conclusion that I was perfectly sane. Dr. Denham, in particular, conversed with the other gentlemen with much apparent earnestness, for he had had the opportunity of witnessing my actions for a period of seven years. I was subsequently informed that Dr. Denham had told an official that I was naturally a well-disposed person; but that when I considered I was labouring under a mis-carriage of justice I was inclined to act in a manner that was perfectly uncontrollable.

Doubtless his Excellency Governor Weld had, owing to my unseemly behaviour in his presence, ordered that the examination as to my sanity should be held instead of taking me before a court of justice, where I could have submitted facts in exoneration of my offence.

On the next visit of Governor Weld to the Penitentiary, I expressed my sincere sorrow and regret for the conduct I had 1. .... of towards him on the occasion of his former visit I humbly begged that he would forgive me in accordance with the dictates of his conscience as a Christian gentleman and the teachings of Holy Writ I also prayed that Mr Reibey's promise with regard to my liberty should be fulfilled.

Shortly after this, however, Governor Weld took his departure from Tasmania, without sanctioning the restoration of my liberty.   Moreover, my life from that time became more miserable, for those authorities whom I had reported took every advantage of me, and, in fact, exercised their power against me so much that I was seldom free from trouble

In January, 1882, I made application to the sheriff for permission to petition his Excellency Sir G. C. Strahan, as I was just completing my tenth year of imprisonment Consent was granted, but the reply I received was, that the Governor, with the advice of his Council declined to interfere at that time

In January, 1883, by permission, I again petitioned, the decision of the Executive being that only in the event of good conduct would they consider my case, and as there had been six "convicted" offences recorded against me since 1882, they refused to take any action   This was another false representation, for of the six offences which had been recorded against me, I had been convicted of one only, and for which I received a sentence of twenty-four hours solitary, on bread and water   This mis-statement, therefore, debarred me from obtaining my liberty at that time

In January, 1884, I once more sought leave to petition, but on that occasion the sheriff refused permission to do so until the 20th of March, by which time twelve months would have elapsed since my last breach of the regulations.

Before that time arrived, however, Governor Strahan, accompanied by the admiral of the Australian station, paid a visit to the Penitentiary   I attracted the attention of Governor Strahan, and he crossed over and spoke to me, asking among other things whether I had ever been in the army   I told him that I had enlisted in the Royal Artillery, at Woolwich, on one occasion, but was unable to remain in the regiment, owing to a dislocated ankle. His Excelleincy next asked me my chest measurement, and upon telling him that I did not exactly know, he sent to the tailor's shop for a tape to measure me, at the same time remarking that I must have been a powerful man in my younger days

Before his Excellency left the prison, I took the opportunity of begging him to allow me to detail the circumstances of my case, for his information when I sent in my petition for freedom, and I humbly trusted that when the matter came before him, he would exercise his influence on my behalf   He cheerfully promised to make the necessary investigation, and also see that it received due attention

When the time arrived I prepared my petition and the details I had promised to forward to the Governor, but the sheriff detained the documents until his Excellency had left the island on a visit to Australia. He then returned the documents to me, with strict injunctions that I should not write another petition unless on the grounds of mercy, for he would not forward any more which pleaded justification.

A short time after I drew out another petition in the manner the sheriff had stated, and received a reply from the acting Governor-in-Council to the effect that if I remained two years in prison without committing any offence, I would be released on ticket-of-leave, although I had been under a conditional pardon when I received my sentence for manslaughter in 1872.

I considered this very unsatisfactory, as the Ticket-of-Leave Act had been abolished since 1852, since which time many persons undergoing life sentences had been restored to freedom.

On the 7th of June, 1887, I received twenty-four hours solitary confinement; but from that time until June, 1889, I committed no breach of the regulations. I then respectfully requested the superintendent to apply for my discharge, which he did; but once more the Ministry were against me, and declined to interfere with the sentence, which had then expired according to the decision of the acting Governor-in-Council in the year 1884; but at last, through the influence of some kind gentleman, who interceded for me, I was sent from the Hobart Gaol to the Launceston Invalid Depot, as a ticket-of-leave man, on the 23rd December, 1890.

Here I still remain in a degree of comfort and contentment, living in the fond hope that the freedom my heart has long yearned for will yet be restored to me.

FAREWELL.

Such is my story! I shall perhaps be accused by many of dilating too much on the details of my misdeeds, and, contrary to my general rule, I must plead guilty to the charge; but in order to be explicit I have found it impossible to avoid running a little into extremes.

As I look back along the vistas of vice and crime, in the haunts of which my manhood has been wasted, my soul is torn by the most poignant regrets, and I feel deeply humiliated. Instinctively, I am not a criminal; and, moreover, I firmly express my consciousness of having done no intentional wrong to anybody during my enforced confinement. I have always striven to act fair and square to those who treated me as a man; and the majority of the evil deeds recorded in this book should be charged against those who acted towards me as if—instead of being an offshoot from the same parent stem—I was some unnamed wild beast of the field, having no feelings or desires in common with themselves.

One sentence sums up my life: I have lived long; I have suffered long. Yet now I feel that the same unseen influence which has guided me through the many horrible crises of my life is surely leading me out of this wilderness of sin into a haven of perpetual rest and peace. May it prove so!

Before closing the pages of this book, I wish to express my sincere and lasting gratitude to those humane and Christian gentlemen who have ministered so kindly either to my spiritual or bodily welfare. Their good work has caused me to grow brighter and happier day by day, and I trust that when they "cross the bar" the "Pilot" will greet each one of them with those welcome words I so long to hear myself—"Enter thou into the joy of thy Lord."

With this public expression of my gratitude, I bid my readers a long

FAREWELL!

Wholly set up and printed
in Australia by
TAYLOR & SON,
Russell Place, Melbourne.

CPSIA information can be obtained at www.ICGtesting.com

231686LV00004B/17/P